Moscow's
Lost Empire

Also by Michael Rywkin

Moscow's Muslim Challenge
Soviet Central Asia

Soviet Society Today

Moscow's
Lost Empire

Michael Rywkin

M. E. Sharpe

Armonk, New York ■ London, England

Library of Congress Cataloging-in-Publication Data

Rywkin, Michael.
Moscow's lost empire / Michael Rywkin.
p. cm.
Includes bibliographical references and index.
ISBN 1-56324-236-2.—ISBN 1-56324-237-0 (pbk.)
1. Former Soviet republics—Ethnic relations.
2. Minorities—Former Soviet republics.
3. Soviet Union—Politics and government.
I. Title.
DK33.R97   1993
93-29308
305.8′00947—dc20
CIP

Printed in the United States of America

The paper used in this publication meets the minimum requirements of
American National Standard for Information Sciences—
Permanence of Paper for Printed Library Materials,
ANSI Z 39.48-1984.

Maps prepared by Marc A. Lundy,
On Tour Productions.

∞

BM (c)   10   9   8   7   6   5   4   3   2   1
BM (p)   10   9   8   7   6   5   4   3   2   1

Contents

List of Tables

List of Maps

Preface

A few years ago I published a book titled *Soviet Society Today*, which was intended for readers who wanted solid information about the Soviet Union presented in an easily digestible form. This was done by keeping the chapters short, the language clear, and the notes minimal. Since then the Soviet Union has disintegrated and Soviet society, in the apt words of one observer, has become the society of yesterday. But the national and ethnic problems described in *Soviet Society Today* survived the collapse of the Union, just as they survived seventy years of Soviet power, and have become a key issue in the post-Soviet period.

This development propelled me to start on a new book devoted solely to ethnic and national problems, a book covering the background and the current fate of the principal nationalities assembled under the Romanov crown and later under the Soviet hammer and sickle. The intention is to give the reader a full picture of national and ethnic issues affecting the former Soviet Union and its component republics, or rather their heirs, the post-Soviet states, at the outset of their independent existence. This book does not pretend to compete with either scholarly monographs covering specific aspects of the subject or journalistic essays based on personal observations of current events.

Given the sheer speed of change in the post-Soviet states, the temptation to be fully up-to-date had to be resisted: today's news may be forgotten within a few months. What is important is to distinguish developments with potential long-term impact from passing events. It is the author's hope that *Moscow's Lost Empire* will not only satisfy the reader's curiosity, but will provide solid background for the interpretation of subsequent events and more advanced study.

The enormous cultural variation of the peoples of the former Soviet Union, as well as the long historical period to be covered, made it impossible to give this book the cohesiveness of *Soviet Society Today*. The parts of the book could have been arranged in a different way and indeed can be read in any order. Each reader or instructor will decide how best to suit the book to individual needs.

* * *

This volume could not have been completed without several contributing factors:

(1) My academic trips to the (ex–) Soviet Union in 1984, 1987, 1990, 1992, and 1993, as well as my personal experience of having lived there during World War II;

(2) A richness of personal and academic contacts in Moscow, St. Petersburg, Kiev, Tashkent, Baku, Tbilisi, Erevan, Tallinn, and Vilnius;

(3) My long activity in the Association for the Study of Nationalities (ex-USSR and East Europe) and its journal, *Nationalities Papers*, as well as my association with the Nationalities Seminar of the Harriman Institute of Columbia University in New York, the Center for Ethno-Political Studies of the Foreign Policy Association and the Institute of Ethnology and Anthropology in Moscow, the Shevchenko Scientific Society in New York, and the University of Warsaw's Program on Eastern Europe and Central Asia. I also greatly benefited from professional contacts with individual scholars: Henry Huttenbach, Alexander Motyl, and John Hazard in New York; Roman Szporluk at Harvard; Emil Payin, Viktor Perevedentsev, and Victor Kozlov in Moscow; Marie Bennigsen-Broxup in

London; professors Hélène Carrère d'Encausse in Paris, Andrus Park in Tallinn, Marco Buttino in Torino, Jan Malicki in Warsaw, and many others.

I am grateful to Professor Seymour Becker for reading the draft manuscript and to my daughter Monique for taking care of the initial editing.

Patricia Kolb, executive editor at M.E. Sharpe, Inc., merits special mention since without her benevolent labor this book could never have been completed. She not only took on herself the thankless task of editing and reediting the text, but subjected all its parts to thorough criticism, forcing me to clarify, expand, and revise several chapters.

Moscow's
Lost Empire

Introduction

The Disintegration of
the Soviet Empire

The Soviet empire, heir to that of the tsars, was the last great European empire to succumb to the inevitable. The Ottoman, Habsburg, and Romanov empires had fallen after World War I, and the remaining West European empires after World War II. But the Romanov empire in a new form would manage a second lifetime of seventy-two years.

It was the attraction of the communist ideology that allowed the Russian empire to outlive its peers. True, the recovery of territories lost in the initial disintegration was achieved by military force, but that alone would not have been sufficient. The new Soviet regime offered powerful enticements as well: recognition of the separateness of its many nationalities, formal institutions of national self-government, and the principle of equality of nations within the Union. No longer were the component nations to be treated as simple provinces of Great Russia. The larger nations were granted republic status (as "union" or "autonomous" republics) along with other attributes of statehood: governments, parliaments, ministries (initially called "people's commissariats"), constitutions, codes of law, national anthems, and so forth. The principle that "all nations are equal" was enforced and ethnic discrimination was outlawed. And what is even more important, all the nations of the Soviet Union were to participate in the building of a new society devoid of class exploitation and national antagonisms. Class struggle within a given nation was to replace the struggle between nations, while hostility between the communist and capitalist camps would overshadow all other kinds of confrontation.

The survival of the Russian empire in its new Soviet form was thus due to its communist content. However, the new structure had deficiencies that in time would precipitate its downfall. First of all, the idea that Russia was the "leading nation" was never overcome. Although condemned as "Great Russian chauvinism" during the revolution, this principle was revived a generation later, grew stronger during World War II, and never left the scene again. Thus the New Soviet Man was to speak Russian, "the language of interethnic communication," and serve in a Russian-led army molded by Russian military tradition. He was to relate to Russian history and symbols, and give up forever all dreams of national independence. In compensation, the forms of national sovereignty were respected, national leaders were allowed to exercise their power (though under Russian control), and members of a national group were granted privileged access to education, jobs, and promotion within their own nationality's territory. These policies contributed to national consolidation.

The split personality of the national republics, torn between formal independence and actual dependence on the center, created a reservoir of hostility toward Moscow's rule, coupled with a sense of unfulfilled national ambition. Over time, the failures of the centrally planned economic system undermined the image of Russian competence, while the demographic decline of the Russian nation set limits to the Kremlin's colonial ambitions. Thus all the elements needed for the demise of the Soviet empire were in place, awaiting an appropriate occasion to erupt into the open. That moment came when Mikhail S. Gorbachev, in the pursuit of his liberal reform agenda, removed the threat of physical punishment for non-Party political activity. As nationalist agitation increased, Gorbachev hoped to placate the nations of the USSR by offering limited concessions; but each concession came too late, and the non-Russian nations became increasingly impatient with the limitations on their sovereignty.

In each republic a specific event opened the gate to militant nationalism. For the Baltic republics it was Moscow's condemnation of the Soviet-German Non-Aggression Pact of 1939; in the Caucasus it was the conflict over Nagorno-Karabakh; and for the Kazakhs it was the Alma-Ata riots of December 1986, the ecological disaster of the Aral Sea, and revelations about the effects of nuclear testing on their territory. The courage shown by Baltic nationalists in the first open challenge to Moscow greatly emboldened other republics. When the Soviet military did intervene in Tbilisi, Baku, and Vilnius, causing civilian deaths, the Kremlin won a short-term reprieve at the cost of a drastic worsening of relations between the republics and the center.

The rapidity of the final disintegration of the USSR following the unsuccessful putsch of August 1991 shocked everyone, but the faultlines had been there since the beginning. The empty forms of national autonomy waited only to be filled. When that began to happen during the years of *perestroika*, the "leading nation" was in turmoil and the communist glue had dried up. Nothing could arrest the process of disintegration: it was every nation for itself. The only real surprise was the suddenness of the collapse.

Western sovietology long ago restricted study of Soviet nationalities problems to the sideline, as a sort of fringe specialty. "Kremlinology," the economics of socialism, Marxist-Leninist ideology, party structure, the military and the KGB, literary dissent—all these subjects took priority over ethnic problems, which were viewed as secondary and virtually irrelevant to the stability of the Soviet Union. (Andrei Amalrik's essay *Will the USSR Survive 1984?*, which predicted the disintegration of the Soviet Union, was dismissed as science fiction.)

American sovietologists only rarely distinguished between "Soviet" and "Russian" and typically regarded ethnic relations in terms of federal structure. Thus, George Kennan, in *Russia and the West Under Lenin and Stalin*, used the terms "Soviet people" and "Russian people" interchangeably and gave no hint of potential problems that might be caused by the Soviet Union's ethnic diversity. Merle Fainsod, too, implicitly equated Russia with the USSR. His *How Russia Is Ruled*, the bible for generations of students of Soviet affairs, contains no chapter, or even subchapter, devoted to nationalities, only a few mentions inserted into discussions of administrative divisions and procedures. James Billington's *The Icon and the Axe* referred to Adam Mickiewicz as "the bard of suffering Poland" but relegated Taras Shevchenko to a minor role as a defender of the "Ukrainian peasantry," thus unwittingly accepting the official Soviet class interpretation of Shevchenko's protests.

This pattern persisted well into the Gorbachev years. In *Political Culture and Leadership in Soviet Russia* (1987), Robert Tucker used "Russia" and "Soviet Union" as synonyms and paid no attention whatsoever to nationality issues. Moshe Lewin, in *The Gorbachev Phenomenon* (1988), quoted the Soviet sociologist Ovsei Shkaratan to the effect that ethnic identity and solidarity are "the result of primary, natural, spontaneous historical processes" (p. 96), but drew no conclusions from this point. Lewin's prognostications about the Soviet Union were premised on such factors as urbanization, education, progress since Stalin's death, and an awakening of the Communist Party at the grass roots. Lewin saw the interplay between "groups and classes" as the prime mover in change, yet he ignored nationality problems and their possible impact.

Jerry Hough, in *Russia and the West* (also 1988), did speak of ethnic problems, but he dismissed them as secondary: "It would be a mistake . . . to exaggerate the potential for ethnic instability in the Soviet Union in the near future" (p. 104). "The Soviet leadership has been successful in keeping non-Russians under control. . . . [I]n fact control over the borderlands has been stable." Hough took note of Russia's worries about ethnic tensions, but linked the latter solely to the "impact of economic reforms on nationalities relations" (p. 105).

Gail Lapidus's essay "The Soviet Nationalities Question" (in *The Gorbachev Era*, a 1986 volume edited by Alexander Dallin and Condoleeza Rice) showed more awareness of ethnic factors, but concluded: "the nationality problem creates complex challenges for the Soviet system and the new Soviet leadership, but is unlikely to disrupt the stability of the Soviet system" (p. 82).

This pattern of reductionist thinking among Soviet specialists has many sources. It can be traced, first, to the Russo-centric bias of the three leading Russian émigré historians who found refuge in the United States: George Vernadsky, Michael M. Karpovich, and Michael T. Florinsky. These influential scholars devoted only limited attention to non-Russian nationalities after their conquest by Russia, and kept clear of post-1917 ethnic issues. Another factor was the assumption that the study of national identity belongs to ethnography or anthropology, not to political science, and the hiring decisions of political science departments in the leading American universities reflected this judgment. Specialists on Soviet nationality affairs were presumed to be causists identified with particular ethnic groups—Ukrainian refugees studying Ukrainian problems, Baltic refugees working on Baltic issues, and so forth. Among American scholars who understood the importance of ethnic issues in the Soviet Union, only Richard Pipes achieved prominence. Others, such as Edward Allworth, an expert on Central Asia, remained known only to specialists.

The situation was better in England and in France. Preoccupation with "colonial affairs" remained strong in both countries, and the Algerian War intensified French interest in Soviet Islam. Leading French scholars, including Alexandre Bennigsen, Vincent Monteil, and Chantal Lemercier-Quelquejay, kept Soviet Muslim studies alive, and Hélène Carrère d'Encausse became the first Soviet nationalities expert to command mass attention. Her book *L'Empire éclaté* (*The Shattered Empire*), published in 1978, foresaw the coming disintegration of the Soviet empire! I still remember the laughter of American sovietologists who dismissed her prediction as a sensationalist ploy, concocted to sell the book to a naive audience.

In Great Britain, the old colonial office hand Geoffrey Wheeler kept Central Asian studies alive, a task later assumed by Enders Wimbush and Marie Bennigsen-Broxup. Yet the prominent British scholar Leonard Shapiro in his classic study *The Communist Party of the Soviet Union* (1960) gave only minor attention to the Marxist treatment of nationalism as a "transient force" and some statistics on the ratios of non-Russians among party cadres.

It appears that Western views on Soviet ethnic reality were very much influenced by Soviet propaganda claiming that Moscow had "solved" nationality problems and by official writings coming out of the republics that lauded Soviet rule and the benefits of the Soviet way of life. But even those rare scholars who recognized the reality of Soviet nationality problems made numerous errors in their assessments.

The most important of those errors was the assumption that conflicts among various nationalities were of much less significance than conflicts between the non-Russians and the Russians. Thus, most of the writings on nationality issues concentrated on tensions between the periphery and the center, and between Russians and non-Russians in the republics. Today, of course, it would be difficult to discount the significance of the conflicts pitting Armenians against Azeris or Ukrainians against Moldavians.

Another error shared by a number of experts was the assumption that certain supranational identities—one notable example being Islam—would prevail over national or subnational (tribal) allegiances. Events in Central Asia and the Caucasus have shown that this is not the case. While Islam is a key factor in every one of the Muslim republics, Islamic solidarity has not materialized to the extent of preventing interethnic conflicts, even among Sunnites (Uzbeks, Meskhetian Turks, Kyrgyzes). A similar error was made by Aleksandr Solzhenitsyn and others who never doubted the solidity of the ties linking Russians, Ukrainians, and Belarusians.

Another widespread assumption held that *nomenklatura* interests would prove stronger than ethnic solidarity and that the gap between party elites and masses in the Soviet Union was insurmountable. Again, this was not the case. As party power weakened, national nomenklaturas jettisoned their Kremlin connections and jumped on the nationalist bandwagon. True, the move was not always successful. In the Baltic republics and in Armenia and Georgia, the newly converted national-communists initially lost out to their nationalist challengers. But in most of the Muslim republics, as well as in Ukraine and in Belorussia (now known as Belarus), the communist nomenklatura made a successful transition and managed to keep power, albeit under a different label. To sever ties with Moscow and abandon Marxism-Leninism was no problem: there was never much genuine liking for the authoritarian center; communist ideology had been dead for decades; and party membership signified ambition, not a genuine ideological commitment.

Finally, many students of nationality problems (myself included) shared the belief that the Muslim republics of the Soviet Union would be the first to present a potent challenge to the stability of the Union. Again, this was not the case. If the process of disintegration had taken a few decades longer, the shifting demographic balance and the failure of the center's integrationist efforts might have taken their toll. But that was not the way it happened. It was Eastern Europe's exodus from the Soviet bloc that triggered events, awakening the westernmost Soviet republics first. The three Baltic republics would lead the way, and it was Ukraine whose shift toward independence would end the attempt to reconstruct the Union. Today it appears that the magnetic pull of Europe—of Berlin, Paris, and London, of NATO and the European Common Market—will have the greatest impact on the future of the Soviet successor states.

Future students of nationality problems in the former Soviet Union will have a wide array of issues to deal with: the treatment of minorities within the republics, the fate of Russian settlers, local chauvinist tendencies, the uneven path of market reforms, attempts at economic cooperation and political understanding, Russian nationalist ferment, and many more. All this promises years of uninterrupted occupation for students of nationality affairs. But the educational background of future experts will have to change. Command of local languages will become more important as the use of the Russian *lingua franca* diminishes. Western diplomats will have to learn to deal with the multitude of political formations on the territory of the former USSR—many lacking internal stability—and their changing and shifting inter-relations. The comforts of the old sovietology—a single ideology, a clear center of power, and stable structures—are past. From now on, the area specialist's work will be more varied and interesting, but also much more demanding.

Part 1

Regions

1

The Russian Core

Russia has retreated to its pre-Petrine borders, leaving behind the debris of its fallen empire. "The unshakable union of free republics forged forever by Great Russia" is no more. The enormity of this event, and the rapidity of its unfolding, have created a psychological drama affecting all Russians.

Most Russians were sure of their own predominance within the Soviet multinational structure, and few were conscious of the oppressive character of Russian domination over the "lesser nations." On the contrary, many saw interethnic relations in the country in terms of Russia's sacrifices for the benefit of its junior partners. The country's territorial continuity over the European landmass from Brest to Vladivostok and from Murmansk to Dushanbe seemed quite unlike the classical colonial pattern of a faraway metropolis controlling overseas dependencies. Ideological emphasis on the equality of nations left little room, at least in theory, for colonial relations. Stalin-era violations of those norms were dismissed as past history, irrelevant in present conditions. All the above considerations left Russians with the illusion that everything was basically under control in the realm of interethnic relations, that nationalist agitation in the republics would find limited appeal among the mass of the local population, and that economic concessions would be sufficient to relieve any discontent.

The history of incorporation of other nations into the Russian empire was rewritten after the 1930s to stress the voluntary, progressive character of annexation by Russia. With school texts appropriately altered and contrary views silenced, Russians were disposed to accept the official version of events. Belief that the Russian nation was essentially benevolent overcame any misgivings about the character of Russian expansion. Russia was seen by most Russians as the bearer of science, education, and modernity into the remotest corners of the land. The Russian language was hailed as the carrier of European civilization into the less advanced regions and as the only practical *lingua franca* for the country.

During the process of unraveling of the Soviet Union, and especially after 1988–89, Russian public opinion split into two camps: "empire savers," for whom maintaining the USSR was a priority, and "nation builders" (including Aleksandr Solzhenitsyn), who believed that Russia could only benefit by shedding its costly imperial burden. The most popular argument in favor of decolonization was based on Russian national interest: the dismantling of their empires seemed to lift the standard of living of the capitalist nations and might do the same for Russia—an idea with some appeal for Russia's impoverished masses. Yet most among the second group still envisioned Russia in permanent partnership with Ukraine and Belarus (Belorussia), and not even a small minority foresaw a return to the borders of old Muscovy. When the unthinkable happened, the Russian public reacted with the shock of betrayal. The uncertain fate of the large Russian minorities in most of the republics made acceptance even more difficult.

Every multinational empire in modern history was founded by a leading nation whose dominance ensured the survival of the imperial entity and whose weakening triggered the unraveling process. Russia (or Great Russia, if one uses the traditional definition) played just such a role.

The rise of Russia since the fifteenth century, after the end of

Mongol domination and the beginning of Russia's eastward expansion, happened in several stages. First, Moscow gathered up the old principalities of the defunct Kievan Rus which remained outside the Polish-Lithuanian state. Then came the conquest of Kazan and Astrakhan, two of the three khanates into which the Golden Horde had split. Next was the rapid drive from the Volga into Siberia and on to the Pacific Ocean, an expansion that brought Russia enormous territories and great power status. There followed a three-pronged struggle in the West: against Sweden for access to the Baltic Sea; against Poland for possession of Ukraine and Belarus; and against the Ottoman empire and its Crimean ally for access to the Black Sea, the Caucasus, and the Balkans. The southern drive culminated in the conquest of the Khanate of Crimea and Russian expansion into the North Caucasus and the Transcaucasus, reaching the present-day Turkish and Iranian borders. The final drive was the one into Central Asia, which projected Russian power from the Kazakh steppe to the borders of Chinese Sinkiang, British India, and Afghanistan. Russia's westerly drive reached its furthest point at the borders of Prussia during the eighteenth-century partitions of Poland.

The Russians, while lacking the adventurous spirit of the Spanish or the English with their relish for overseas conquests and colonization, were well suited for overland expansion. The imperial idea of Muscovy as the "Third Rome," the final heir to the Roman empire and Byzantium, with its mission to rule over smaller and weaker nations and uncivilized *inorodtsy* (a term applied to the non-Christians of the empire), took hold at the turn of the fifteenth century. The concept of the superiority of the Russian Orthodox faith over other religions, especially non-Christian ones, was the second component of the Russian colonial mentality. The third component was a pride in the Russian people's ability to endure physical hardships and its fighting spirit (*udal*), and a belief that Russia's human resources were inexhaustible.

Holding the empire together, finally, was the iron hand of Russian autocracy, personified in the tsar as the absolute master of the land. Russia's rulers, unlike those in Warsaw or old Novgorod, were accountable to no one and required neither approval nor consent.

When the pinnacle of imperial expansion was reached at the end of the nineteenth century, dangers were looming. Russia's defeat in the 1904–5 Russo-Japanese War and the revolutionary uprising of 1905 subdued expansionist ambitions. Losses in World War I and the successive revolutions of February and October 1917 led to imperial collapse. By 1919 Russian-held territory was reduced to the borders of four centuries before. But soon the process of disintegration was arrested and most of Russia's imperial possessions were brought under Soviet power. This was accomplished by a combination of far-reaching concessions to non-Russian nationalities, appeals to the revolutionary zeal of the toiling masses, and, at appropriate moments, the application of sheer force. Within the newly established federal state, the Russians were to be no longer the official masters but rather "first among equals," although once more they were the human fabric holding the renamed empire together. Non-Russian leaders—numerous and powerful in the period of revolution and civil war—eventually fell into obscurity, except of course for Iosif Stalin, a Georgian by birth, who during the decades of his rule would increasingly rely on Russian patriotism as a substitute for waning revolutionary enthusiasm. In the face of the German attack and occupation during World War II, it would be the supreme effort of the Russian people that made victory possible and maintained the empire intact for another half-century.

Yet throughout the Soviet period, the vitality of the Russian nation was slowly being sapped. After the revolution the cream of the Russian aristocracy, military, clergy, and merchant class was either exterminated or driven into exile (the lucky ones reached the West; others went to Siberia). Soviet social experiments, from forced collectivization and rapid industrialization to bloody purges and endless punishments and deprivations, followed by the German invasion and subsequently by a new wave of Stalinist repressions, gravely compromised Russia's vaunted strength. In the Soviet experiment the Russian nation was used as both tool and expendable commodity.

Most other nations of the USSR preserved their vitality and national spirit more successfully than the Russians did. They did so by perceiving communist social experimentation as Russian-planned and Russian-imposed, and therefore an ordeal not of their own making. The experience of common suffering increased national cohesiveness even between the officials and the masses, to the extent that officials could be seen to serve as protectors against Moscow's excesses.

The Russians, on the other hand, were being molded into a kind of de-ethnicized Soviet filler, deprived of national consciousness except when useful to the state, as during the war years. In the postwar period, the decline of Russian demographic vitality accelerated, as evidenced by their low birthrate, decreased longevity among Russian men, widespread alcoholism, high divorce rate, and frequent debility among youth. What was left of the Russian work ethic, simple peasant tenacity, and personal initiative succumbed to the combined forces of bureaucratization, homogenization, indifference, and stagnation. Thus, while the national consciousness of non-Russian nationalities was submerged, the Russians alone found themselves, often to their own dismay, assuming the identity of denationalized "Soviets."

Gorbachev's policy of glasnost, which opened the possibility of national self-expression to all the peoples of the USSR, did the same for the Russians. While other nations blamed the Russians for their misfortunes, the Russians, in turn, sought familiar culprits in Jews, Masons, minorities, and their own supposed excessive generosity toward alien nations both inside and outside the USSR. The old Slavophile doctrine of rejecting Western ideas, particularly those of freedom and democracy, resurfaced. At the same time, the desire to hold on to the empire at all costs became a rallying point for conservative forces. Thus in Russia today the political right includes such diverse groups as old-school Stalinists, great power militarists, and new-style "Black Hundreds" (among them the group *Pamiat*, which in Russian means

Table 1

National Composition of the Population of the USSR in 1979 and 1989
(nationality groups in descending order of size in 1989)

	1979 (in 000)	1989 (in 000)	% increase 1979–1989
Total USSR	262,085	285,689	9.0
Russians	137,397	145,072	5.6
Ukrainians	42,347	44,136	4.2
Uzbeks	12,466	16,686	31.0
Belorussians	9,462	10,030	6.0
Kazakhs	6,556	8,138	24.1
Azerbaijanis	5,477	6,791	24.0
Tatars	6,185	6,646	7.4
Armenians	4,151	4,627	11.5
Tajiks	2,898	4,217	45.5
Georgians	3,571	3,983	11.6
Moldavians	2,698	3,355	13.0
Lithuanians	2,851	3,068	7.6
Turkmen	2,028	2,718	34.0
Kyrgyzes	1,906	2,531	32.8
Peoples of Daghestan	1,657	2,072	25.1
Germans	1,936	2,036	5.1
Chuvash	1,751	1,839	5.0
Latvians	1,439	1,459	1.4
Bashkirs	1,371	1,449	5.7
Jews	1,811	1,449	-20.0
Mordvins	1,192	1,154	-3.2
Poles	1,151	1,027	-2.2
Estonians	1,020	1,027	0.7

	1979	1989	% change
Kara-Kalpaks	303	423	39.6
Buryats	353	422	19.6
Kabardians	322	395	22.7
Yakuts	328	382	16.5
Bulgarians	361	379	4.9
Greeks	344	358	4.1
Chechens	756	958	26.8
Udmurts	714	747	4.6
Maris	622	670	7.8
Ossetians	542	598	10.3
Komi/Komi-Permiaks	477	497	4.1
Koreans	389	437	12.4
Crimean Tatars	132	269	103.2
Uigurs	211	262	24.5
Gypsies	209	262	25.2
Ingush	186	238	27.6
Turks	93	207	123.0
Tuvinians	166	207	24.6
Peoples of the North	158	197	24.6
Gagauz	173	197	13.8
Kalmyks	147	175	19.0
Hungarians	171	172	0.8
Karachai	131	156	19.1
Kurds	116	153	32.0
Romanians	129	146	13.3
Karelians	138	131	-5.1
Adygei	109	125	14.9
Abkhaz	91	102	13.2

Source: 1979 and 1989 censuses.
Note: Ethnic groups counting less than 100,000 persons not listed.

"memory"). However vocal and colorful it may be, the Russian right still constitutes a minority among the Russian population. It is, nevertheless, a dangerous minority, capable of growing if reforms fail and popular frustration increases the attraction of an authoritarian solution. The success of Vladimir Zhirinovsky's "Liberal Democratic" Party in the parliamentary elections of December 1993 was a powerful indicator of the right's appeal.

Russian reformist forces, which have managed to hold on to their position of influence under the aegis of President Boris Yeltsin, are led by intellectuals and members of the new middle class. They are drawn to Western prosperity and ideals, and see little advantage in efforts to restore a fractious empire. They were impatient with the seemingly slow pace of reforms under Gorbachev and wanted to speed the process of transition from a planned economy and regulated society to a market economy in a freely developing society. By 1993, however, the hard economic realities of postcommunist reconstruction had cooled the commitment of many former reform enthusiasts; the reformers' split into several competing factions was reflected in the December election results.

The bulk of the Russian population, the "swing vote" that can go either way, is primarily concerned about its material well-being and personal security. It is still too early to judge whether Russians' willingness to defend freedom in August 1991 (and the unwillingness of the army to be used against the Russian people) signifies a permanent shift away from the traditional Russian acceptance of oppression. Although Russians quickly learned to appreciate their newly acquired freedoms, many are understandably inclined to blame reformers for the country's severe economic and social transition pains.

2

Ukraine and Belarus

The history of Russia's "younger brothers," Ukraine and Belarus (as Belorussia now prefers to be known), is closely connected with the history of not only Russia but also Poland and Lithuania.

Both Ukraine and Belarus originated in Kievan Rus, the mother of the three eastern Slavic nations. At the time of the christening of Kievan Rus in the tenth century, differences among the tribes that later evolved into separate nations were not great.

It was the Tatar invasion of the early thirteenth century that began the split. Initially all of Kievan Rus, except for its northernmost part, succumbed to the invader. Later, the lands of present-day Ukraine and Belarus passed into the hands of the pagan, but tolerant, Lithuanians. In the fourteenth century Lithuania joined Poland and accepted Christianity. In the sixteenth century, Ukraine came under Polish rule, while Belarus remained with Lithuania until the dissolution of the Polish-Lithuanian Commonwealth at the end of the eighteenth century. Thus the old principalities of Kievan Rus followed separate paths. Those that were to form Muscovite Russia remained under Tatar domination for centuries while Belarus and Ukraine enjoyed the relative freedom prevailing in the Polish-Lithuanian state.

In the fifteenth century, free of Tatar rule, Muscovy began to expand, emerging as the heir to Kievan Rus. At the same time,

Polish magnates, whose enormous estates in the eastern border-lands remained autonomous from Warsaw's rule, got more power over their Ukrainian and Belarusian subjects.

The Ukrainian road to nationhood began in the borderlands between Poland, Russia, and Crimea. As the Tatars retreated, the steppe was resettled by Cossacks—men of arms, adventurers, and runaways, who sought refuge from Moscow serfdom in this no-man's-land, where they lived off hunting, fishing, and armed forays. As they became stronger and more numerous, they attracted new adherents, established families, and began tilling the land. The Cossacks began to resent the power of the Polish magnates, who, in an effort to protect their own domains, tried to bring the Cossacks under tighter control.

It was during the eighteenth-century wars waged by the Cossacks against the decentralized Polish state that Ukrainian national consciousness first emerged. The peasantry, sometimes against their will, joined the Cossacks under hetman Bohdan Khmelnytsky in fighting the Poles (and slaughtering Jews, who often acted as middlemen between the peasants and the Polish landowners). It was Khmelnytsky's decision to seek Moscow's protection against Warsaw that sealed the fate of Ukraine. Instead of remaining the vassals of weak Polish kings in a rather tolerant and decentralized state, the Cossacks soon found themselves subjects of the Russian autocracy.

Initially, Moscow tolerated Cossack liberties, but soon reneged and began to tighten its hold on eastern Ukraine: serfdom was reaffirmed, Russian nobles were given land grants, and Cossack elders were brought to heel. The hetman was no longer elected, but appointed. After being broken by Tsar Peter the Great, the Cossacks were resettled by Catherine the Great further to the east, in the Don region, where they became instruments of Russia's colonial expansion. New Cossack "voiskas" (territorial units, known in Russian as "armies") were created in the North Caucasus, the Urals, Siberia, and southern Kazakhstan.

After the fall of Crimea and the removal of the Cossacks, Ukrainian lands were reduced to mere provinces of the Russian empire. Ukrainians were not recognized as a separate nationality; they were referred to as "Little Russians," the younger brothers of the dominant "Great Russians." The Russian language and culture replaced Polish, and Ukrainian was considered a dialect, appropriate for peasant chatter and popular songs, but nothing more. With the partition of Poland, the remaining Ukrainian lands west of the Dnieper River were incorporated into the Russian empire, leaving only eastern Galicia, annexed by Austria-Hungary, beyond St. Petersburg's reach.

Belarus ("White Rus"), which, following the partition of Poland, was fully annexed by the Russian empire, has been subjected to even more intense russification than Ukraine. Lacking Ukraine's Cossack tradition and a refuge beyond Russia's reach (the role played by Ukrainian eastern Galicia), Belarus offered less resistance to Russian cultural inroads. When the estates of many Polish nobles were expropriated after two unsuccessful revolts (1830 and 1863), Russian landowners moved in, reinforcing Russian cultural and linguistic dominance. All this delayed Belarusian national renewal until the turn of the twentieth century.

Despite an 1876 imperial decree that prohibited the printing or importing of Ukrainian books, Ukraine did experience a national-cultural revival, especially in Galicia and in Kiev. The fame of such Ukrainian poets as Taras Shevchenko confirmed the distinctiveness of the Ukrainian language and culture. Ukrainian historiography appeared, stressing the separate path of Ukrainian history and condemning "Russian historical imperialism." Tsarist crackdowns drove these Ukrainian cultural activities underground and to neighboring Galicia.

A score of Ukrainian nationalists were elected to the first *Duma* (parliament) in 1906. By the time of the October Revolution, Ukraine was ready to reclaim its independence. It did so in 1918, but Moscow soon managed to reintegrate both Ukraine and Belarus into its fold, albeit as "union republics" within the newly formed Soviet Union. However, the western Ukrainian and Belarusian lands remained within the reborn Polish state, which had managed to recover a part of its eighteenth-century eastern possessions despite a brief confrontation with Moscow in 1920.

During the postrevolutionary years, both Ukraine and Belarus met a common fate familiar to students of Soviet history: an initial terror during the civil war, a relaxation during the period of Lenin's New Economic Policy, and a short-lived attempt at a policy of *korenizatsiia*, or nativization (promotion of native cadres, languages, and cultures in non-Russian areas). The Stalin era brought a ruthless campaign to collectivize peasant agriculture, backed up by deportations of the more prosperous peasant families—so-called kulaks—into Siberia and Central Asia. There ensued widespread famine, successive purges, and finally the tragedy of the German invasion. Any hopes that German occupation might bring relief proved to be short-lived. War brought more devastation, more deportations, and further population losses, alleviated only by the acquisition of western borderlands from Poland and Czechoslovakia in the postwar settlement.

Although the post-Stalin years were milder in many respects, the policies of Stalin's successors continued to erode the vitality of rural society. To further the goal of "erasing the differences between town and countryside," villages were emptied, churches destroyed, and private-plot agriculture curtailed. Ukraine and Belarus experienced cultural and linguistic russification, ecological damage, and economic stagnation. Ukraine, the traditional breadbasket of Europe, turned into yet another example of communist failure. On the positive side, urbanization and education fostered the growth of a Soviet-style middle class.

As fellow Slavs, the Ukrainians and Belarusians enjoyed Moscow's favor as "younger brothers" who could be entrusted with important positions in the Soviet state, the Communist Party, and the military (especially as non-commissioned officers). In the non-Slavic republics of Central Asia, the Caucasus, and the Baltic, they were regarded as virtually interchangeable with Russians, and could be relied upon to support the center against the periphery.

Present-day Ukrainian nationalism is a complex phenomenon.

Table 2

Belarusians and Ukrainians Residing in the Former Soviet Republics (1989)

Republic(s)	Belarusian population (in 000)	Ukrainian population (in 000)
Ukraine	440	37,419
Belorussia	7,905	291
Russian Federation	1,206	4,363
(in Moscow)	(71)	(247)
Kazakhstan	183	896
Central Asian (4 republics)	54	338
Baltic (3 republics)	214	185
Transcaucasian (3 republics)	6	39
Moldavia	20	600

Source: Etnopolis, 1992, nos. 1 and 2 (based on the 1989 census as edited by Mikhail N. Guboglo).

Within Ukraine itself, the intensity of nationalist sentiment varies by region. Dominant in the west, strong in the center, it is much weaker in the east and in the south, where Russians constitute a large minority of the population. This pattern corresponds to historical and cultural differences. Although by religion the Ukrainians, like the Russians, are predominantly Orthodox, Roman Catholics and Uniates (Eastern-rite Catholics who recognize the authority of the Pope) make up significant minorities. These last two groups, among whom nationalist feelings are strongest, were formed under Polish and Austrian influence and remained mostly beyond Moscow's grasp until 1939. The areas of Ukraine that have been associated with Russia the longest have traditionally been less nationalist. Nevertheless, during the Gorbachev years, the new Ukrainian nationalist movement "Rukh" gained support even in the east and south and in such russified cities as Kharkov. Initially concerned with Ukrainian cultural revival, Rukh soon adopted a full-scale nationalist agenda. Resentment against Moscow grew out of a whole array of historic grievances, but was catalyzed by the tragic nuclear accident at Chernobyl.

The Chernobyl disaster, which contaminated the southeastern section of Belarus, had a similar effect on that republic as well. Belarus has traditionally been less nationalist than Ukraine, although, following the Ukrainian pattern, nationalism is stronger in the western part of the country, in areas that were part of the Polish state between the two world wars. Linguistic russification has been more widespread in Belarus: the educational system was fully russified, and acceptance of a common fate with Russia seemed deeply rooted. In addition to the Chernobyl catastrophe, it was the example of neighboring Lithuania, the proximity of Poland, and finally the Ukrainian communists' adoption of a nationalist platform that spurred the Belarusian Communist Party apparatus to follow suit. Even so, independent Belarus has been open to much closer cooperation with Moscow than Ukraine is ready to accept.

Ironically, it was the communist leadership of Ukraine that declared the country fully independent in 1991. Former Communist Party First Secretary Leonid Kravchuk, now president of independent Ukraine, has pursued a four-pronged policy:

1. Independence from Moscow in the pursuit of currency reform and trade policy and a willingness to stand up to Moscow to defend Ukrainian claims to the Crimean peninsula and the Black Sea fleet. Kravchuk has established his nationalist credentials in these public stands. Behind closed doors, however, he is reportedly much more cooperative with Moscow.

2. A "good neighbor" policy with Ukraine's western neighbors and as much contact as possible with the European Economic Community as well as with the United States and Canada (where many Ukrainians reside).

3. Protection of the old communist nomenklatura by leaving them in charge of economic reform, on the grounds that they have the necessary professional expertise. Although the same pattern prevails to some extent in Russia, it is far stronger in Ukraine, with the result that economic reform has made little progress there.

4. Avoidance of conflicts with the Russian minority. Both Ukraine and Belarus opted for a policy of full acceptance of the Russian populations that have lived in their midst for generations.

This policy of national assertiveness balanced by social compromise has proven fairly successful, at least in the short run. The future, however, is much less certain. The key issue of relations with Moscow is bound to come back many times. The reality of Russian economic might, and especially Russia's riches in energy and raw materials, might tempt Moscow to exercise more pressure than Kiev is ready to tolerate. Continuous economic difficulties could ignite nationalist feelings, upsetting the existing *modus vivendi* between Russians and Ukrainians within Ukraine, and between Russia and Ukraine in their post-Soviet coexistence. Political divisions within Ukraine itself, compounded by regional differences, could also lead to instability. Thus the danger of a Yugoslav scenario cannot be ruled out entirely.

The internal political situation in Ukraine is marked by a general agreement among the key factions concerning the essential conditions for Ukrainian statehood: full citizenship for the Russian minority, a precondition for ethnic peace; no Czech-style "lumination" ("shedding light" on public figures' past activities); and restoration of old ties with Eastern Europe, severed during centuries of Russian domination. Twice before in their history the Ukrainians—a nation the size of the French—were within reach of statehood: in the seventeenth century and in 1918–19. The third opportunity presented itself in 1991, and this time Ukraine will not let it slip away.

3

The Baltic West

The three Baltic states reached a common destination by different historic roads.

The largest of the Baltic states, Lithuania, also has the most impressive history. At the high point of its territorial expansion in the fourteenth century, the Grand Duchy of Lithuania was probably the largest country in Europe. It absorbed the western principalities of Kievan Rus that escaped Mongol domination, and stretched from modern East Prussia in the west to Smolensk in the east, and from Riga in the north to the Khanate of Crimea in the south. It included all of present-day Belarus, all the settled area of Ukraine, and even a chunk of Russia proper, west of Moscow.

Lithuania was a tolerant country. Belarusian nobility was accepted on equal terms, and state documents were written in Belarusian. It was only after the "personal union" with Poland, when the Catholic Polish queen Jadwiga married Lithuanian grand duke Jagiello, bringing Christianity to pagan Lithuania, that the Belarusian language was replaced by Polish.

The Polish-Lithuanian Commonwealth was successful in stopping the advance of the Teutonic Knights in the fifteenth century and Tsar Ivan the Terrible's troops in the sixteenth. Eventually the personal union with Poland was transformed into a union of the two states, and the territories of Ukraine passed from Lithuanian into Polish hands. Still, Lithuania remained a partner and not a subject in the Polish-Lithuanian Commonwealth. Once the originally Lithuanian Jagiellonian dynasty had come to an end, the great Lithuanian noble families made their voices heard in elections of Polish kings. In the eighteenth-century partition of the Polish-Lithuanian state, Poland was divided among Prussia, Austro-Hungary, and Russia; Lithuania fell entirely into Russian hands, and became yet another outlying province of the Romanovs' vast empire. By that time most of the Lithuanian nobility had been polonized, and use of the Lithuanian language was preserved mainly among peasants. Only in the nineteenth century did Lithuania experience its own national revival: Lithuanian nationalists no longer sought the restoration of the old partnership with Poland, but a separate design for Lithuania.

Unlike Lithuania, Latvia knew no independent existence prior to the interwar period. Its capital, Riga, founded by Germans in the thirteenth century, became a port in the German-speaking Hanseatic League. In the sixteenth century, Latvian territory was divided between the Polish-Lithuanian state and the kingdom of Sweden. With the ascension of Russia under Peter the Great, a part of Latvia passed into Russian hands. The rest was annexed during the eighteenth-century partition of Poland.

Thus Latvia found itself divided between the Catholic, Protestant, and Eastern Orthodox faiths. Although as a port city, Riga, unlike Vilnius, was always international, the German cultural influence prevailed. It is only during the nineteenth century that Latvian national culture emerged, preparing the country for its future independence.

Unlike the Lithuanians and Latvians, who are distinctive peoples ethnically and linguistically, the Estonians speak a Finno-Ugric language and are closely related to the Finnic tribes that historically inhabited the north of today's European Russia and Finland itself.

Like the Latvians, the Estonians prior to the interwar period never succeeded in forming a state of their own. They fell under

Danish, German, and Swedish influence, until their annexation by Peter the Great in the early eighteenth century. But although they were held in the Russian fold longer than their two Baltic neighbors, the Estonians remained very much outside the Russian cultural sphere, the country being dominated by Baltic German nobility (not unlike the situation in neighboring Latvia). Thus nineteenth-century Estonian nationalists were trying to free themselves from German, rather than Russian, cultural influence.

The Bolsheviks gave up the Romanov empire's Baltic possessions in March 1918, when they signed a separate peace with Germany at Brest-Litovsk. Revolutionary Russia was then forced to recognize the independence of the three Baltic states when World War I ended. Freed from Russian domination, independent Lithuania—minus Vilnius, but plus Klaipeda (the port city of Memel, acquired from East Prussia)—lasted barely twenty years. Lithuania had quickly found itself at odds with its Polish former partner on the thorny question of Vilnius. In their old capital city, Lithuanians were outnumbered by both Poles and Jews. Lithuania lost the city to the reborn Polish state in 1920, but recovered it twenty years later, when Stalin offered Vilnius to Lithuania prior to annexing the country.

Latvia and Estonia, unburdened by territorial disputes with their neighbors, did better at managing their economic affairs, and reached Finnish standards of living by the 1930s. Politically, the little Baltic states were initially part of the French-organized "*cordon sanitaire*," intended to isolate Soviet Russia; but later they flirted with Hitler's Germany and shifted from democratic to authoritarian forms of government.

The Soviet-German Non-Aggression Pact of August 1939 (the Molotov-Ribbentrop Pact) ended the independent existence of the three Baltic states. Latvia and Estonia were assigned to the Soviet sphere. Lithuania (except for Klaipeda), originally assigned to Germany, was traded by Hitler to Stalin in exchange for the Lublin province of Poland. Shortly thereafter, under Soviet pressure, the three Baltic states were forced to accept the stationing of Soviet troops on their territory. In the summer of 1940, these troops staged coups and installed puppet regimes which "asked" for integration with the USSR. Only Finland, larger and strategically better located, dared to oppose Soviet aggression during the winter of 1939–40, and, despite the unequal confrontation, managed to maintain its independence, losing only a small part of its territory.

After 1939, Lithuania, Latvia, and Estonia suffered similar fates: mass deportations to Siberia and Kazakhstan; conquest by Germany at the outset of the German invasion of the USSR in 1941; initial collaboration with the Germans, gradually weakened by Berlin's refusal to restore the Baltic states to their previous status; and finally, reconquest by the Red Army. This was followed by new deportations, guerrilla resistance, forced collectivization, and the arrival of numerous Russian settlers in the area. Originally, the settlers were bought in to consolidate Moscow's hold on the republics, but later they were attracted by the possibility to enjoy higher living standards and a more Western way of life. The construction of large factory complexes brought new waves of Russian settlers as well as ecological damage to the region. Still, despite all the negatives, the Baltic republics managed to keep their national spirit and to maintain a standard of living higher than anywhere else in the Soviet Union. A visitor to Tallinn was struck by the image of a basically Western country, clean, organized, and hard working, although mired in an alien empire that was disorganized and inefficient.

Fifty years of Soviet occupation brought drastic changes in the demographic picture of the Baltic states. While in Lithuania, Russian settlers account for less than 10 percent of the population, in Estonia they reach almost one-third, and in Latvia they constitute over 40 percent of the total. In Latvia and Estonia the "old" Russians, those whose families lived in the country prior to World War II, had no problem integrating into the local life, but the majority of new, "Soviet" Russians ignored the local culture, spoke only Russian, and have shown hostility to the host country's national aspirations.

Real independence for the three little Baltic republics came after the collapse of the August 1991 Moscow putsch. Yet during the two to three preceding years, Soviet presence and local sovereignty had coexisted, however imperfectly. Broad political coalitions under the common umbrella of nationalist "popular fronts" united the bulk of the native population. National-communists aligned themselves with the fronts. On the opposite side were pro-Moscow communist factions, the Soviet military, and hardline Russian settlers' organizations united in so-called interfronts ("internationalist" fronts). Contacts between the opposing sides were limited. Only sporadic clashes, mostly Kremlin-instigated, reminded people that they were not yet free of Soviet control.

Initially enthusiastic about the revival of national symbols and the restoration of national self-esteem, little by little the local populations grew more cynical, and more preoccupied with economic difficulties. Thus, when independence really came, popular enthusiasm was rather subdued. On the one hand, the three republics had already tasted the fruits of independence, despite the Russians' physical presence; on the other, it was clear that the economic costs of independence were going to be much higher than expected, and integration into the world economy far more difficult. The November 1992 victory of the nationalist faction of the former Lithuanian Communist Party under Brazauskas over the Sajudis national front led by Landsbergis was symptomatic of the primacy of economic issues.

An array of problems plague the newborn states. First, the withdrawal of Soviet troops (now under Russian control) has proceeded very slowly. Moscow cites the lack of housing for the returning soldiers and concern about legal discrimination against the Russian minority, arguments that Latvian and Estonian authorities reject as irrelevant to the issue. Another problem is the high cost of energy, since Russia is no longer willing to supply oil and gas at below-market prices. A third problem is the disrup-

Table 3

Ethnic Composition of the Baltic States (1989)

	Lithuania		Latvia		Estonia	
	(000)	(%)	(000)	(%)	(000)	(%)
Titular nationality	2,924	(79.6)	1,388	(52.0)	963	(61.5)
Russians	344	(9.4)	906	(34.0)	475	(30.3)
Ukrainians and Belarusians	108	(2.9)	212	(8.0)	76	(4.9)
Poles[a]	258	(7.0)	60	(2.3)		
Others[b]	41	(1.1)	101	(3.7)	51	(3.3)

Source: 1989 census.

[a]Poles are included with "others" in the data for Estonia.

[b]The total number of Jews in the three Baltic republics combined was approximately 40 thousand.

tion of ties with longtime customers and suppliers located in other former Soviet republics. The erection of state borders, a lack of hard currency, declines in production, and spiraling inflation are some of the causes of this situation. Still more serious barriers to economic recovery are the lack of private capital, disrepair of the housing stock, the inadequate communications infrastructure, obsolete industrial installations, and extensive zones of ecological damage, to list only a few. And finally, there is the psychological legacy of two generations of Soviet life: bureaucratic habits, welfare expectations, atrophy of individual initiative, lack of business acumen, low productivity, and high levels of graft and theft.

4

Muslim Central Asia

Soviet Central Asia together with Kazakhstan covers a larger area than Ukraine and is equal to Ukraine in population. But despite a shared political past, this region is a world apart from the rest of the former Soviet Union. It is of the Orient in its climate, history, ethnicity, and most of all its culture and religion. What is Western is recent (in historical terms), brought by Russia, already altered in a Russian way, and poorly matched with what was before. Except for a few public buildings, modern structures are made of standard Soviet cement blocks, dirty and chipped. Tin roofs replace the traditional flat clay ones in the villages, and bland, official-looking storefronts face what is left of the lively oriental bazaars. Central Asian oases are overpopulated, and child mortality is sky-high. The ecological situation is catastrophic: the soil is damaged by extensive cotton cultivation and chemical fertilization; water reserves are dwindling; the Aral Sea is almost dead.

Central Asian history is ancient and rich. The area experienced endless invasions—Chinese, Arabic, Mongol, even a foray by Alexander the Great. Some of these reshaped the original Aryan and Turkic character of the region, while others, like the Chinese, left barely a trace. In the Middle Ages, the silk road from China led through Central Asia, bringing prosperity, and Iranian influence permeated the local culture. The lush oases of Bukhara and

Samarkand became centers of a flourishing Muslim civilization, rivaling Teheran and Isfahan. Their decline came with the demise of the silk road once European frigates were able to reach the Orient by the sea route around the Cape. The feudal states of Central Asia—the Emirate of Bukhara and the khanates of Khiva and Kokand—never recovered from the loss of commerce and began to stagnate. Still, protected from the north by the seemingly impassable Kazakh steppe and deserts, from the south and east by mountain chains, and from the west by the Caspian Sea, they felt relatively safe from outside interference. The perceived dangers were from Teheran or Kabul, not from faraway London or Moscow.

By the nineteenth century, the Europeans had finally reached the Central Asian interior: the British from India, in an attempt to penetrate Afghanistan, and the Russians through their gradual absorption of the Kazakh steppe and the consequent submission of the three Kazakh hordes.

When in the 1860s the Central Asian khanates felt the impact of Russia's southward drive, they were utterly unprepared to repel it. Lacking political coherence, modern armies, or organizational skills, they were conquered within ten years, pacified within another ten, and finally estranged from the East and absorbed into a new, Russian-dominated empire. Still, tsarist Russia, although it kept the area under tight military control and economic dependence, did not attempt to interfere in everyday life and essentially respected the ways and traditions of the indigenous population. Russia also allowed two states, Bukhara and Khiva, to remain autonomous under their old rulers, albeit reduced in size and under St. Petersburg's protection.

European colonization started soon after the conquest. Some of the fertile lands in the Kazakh steppe were transferred to Cossack hands, driving the nomads away. In the cities of Central Asia, Russian settlers, bureaucrats, railroad workers, and merchants began to arrive, building "new towns" alongside the old native ones, just as the French did in North Africa.

It was the Soviet regime that brought radical changes in the native way of life. After the Bolshevik revolution, a Soviet government was established in Tashkent. Enjoying little native support, the new regime faced prolonged guerrilla warfare with Muslim *basmachi* (counterparts of Afghani *mujahedin*). Having overcome the guerrillas with military force and ruthless pacification measures, the regime began to redraw the borders of the area. This policy of "national delimitation" erased traditional boundaries and established Soviet republics based on the identity of a "titular nationality." Whereas the old multiethnic khanates were united by ruling dynasties and feudal allegiances, the new units were supposed to separate the ethnic groups and provide each with an official homeland. The measure broke the unity of Central Asia and created artificial divisions. Nevertheless, as in today's Africa, over time these colonial borders shaped new allegiances and created new political realities.

The Soviets also undertook to reform the traditional way of life in Central Asia. The usual communist social experiments were carried on without regard for local conditions: confiscation of religious property, forced collectivization, liquidation of kulaks (locally known as *bais*), industrialization, and so forth. The forced settlement of nomads, carried out at the time of collectivization, proved disastrous to local cattle-breeding, while over-cultivation of cotton soon strained the limited water resources of Central Asian oases.

Undercutting the influence of Islam was another goal of the Soviet regime. Mosques were closed and mullahs persecuted. Mosque attendance by Soviet employees was strongly discouraged. Ritual fasts, prayers, circumcisions, marriage ceremonies, and burials were frowned upon. Women were granted legal equality; the wearing of veils was discouraged; polygamy was outlawed; the old customs of child marriage and *kalym* (payment for the bride) were prohibited; and the education of girls was promoted. These measures achieved mixed success. Although many Central Asian Muslims learned to drink and swear and avoided mosques, essential traditions were never completely uprooted. While the Muslim clergy was drastically reduced in numbers, tightly controlled, and compelled to serve state interests, an unofficial clergy filled the gap. Islam was never successfully eradicated from everyday life.

The native party apparatus, which underwent successive purges throughout the 1930s, was outwardly subservient to Moscow. Local party officials learned Russian, operated in a Soviet milieu, and professed allegiance to communist ideals. They remained, however, attached to their traditional ways. Indeed, their distinctive style of rule merged the oriental and the bureaucratic Soviet "command-and-control" models. They favored their own kin, formed local cliques, and saw themselves as protectors of their countrymen against the whims of the Kremlin, but also exploited their power for their own benefit. Moscow tolerated local nepotism and graft in exchange for submission to its directives. An atmosphere of inefficiency and corruption prevailed for years, especially during the "period of stagnation" (1970s and early 1980s). Bribes were universally taken, public offices and academic diplomas sold, collective and state farms milked, factory production misappropriated, commerce corrupted, construction sites robbed of building materials, and nepotism taken for granted.

By 1984, the level of corruption in Central Asia had become too much for Moscow to tolerate and the area was hit with a deluge of investigations. The purge of 1984–88, initiated by Yuri Andropov, continued through Konstantin Chernenko's short rule and acquired fresh momentum during the first years of Gorbachev's leadership. The "anticorruption" drive took the following forms: scores of officials, predominantly natives, were jailed, fired, or demoted. "Clean" Russians, labeled "mature" cadres, were "parachuted" into the republics to replace their obviously "immature" counterparts. Younger, less well connected native bureaucrats were promoted to the remainder of the jobs left vacant, to the great consternation of the old bosses' protégés. In some cases, successive purges affected three "generations" of officeholders, each fired within a year or two after initial appointment.

The purge finally exhausted itself by 1988: the practical results were meager and the consequences heavy. First of all, the Soviet system simply could not function without the "lubrication" provided by corruption. Second, the national nomenklatura considered the opportunity to enrich itself to be due compensation for its allegiance to Moscow, a part of the tacit agreement between the center and the periphery. Moreover, the Moscow bosses had taken their share: corruption was not limited to the locals. Finally, the tradition of *bakshish* (bribery) was an old and accepted way of doing business in Central Asia, and did not provoke much public indignation.

The anticorruption drive was reinforced with anti-Islamic propaganda. The purged native bosses were routinely charged with favoring Islam, protecting Sufi brotherhoods, or siphoning funds to unofficial mosques. Such allegations only increased popular sympathy for the purged officials. The mass importation of Russian officials, ignorant of local languages and customs, was also bound to backfire. The Alma-Ata riots of 1986, which took place after the replacement of the First Secretary of the Communist Party of Kazakhstan, Dinmuhamed Kunaev, by a Russian outsider, Gennadii Kolbin, were an early warning of coming dangers. The last time such a massive influx of Russian cadres into Central Asia had taken place was in the 1940s. But that was under Stalin's iron rule and justified by war emergencies, conditions absent in the 1980s.

The purges failed to eradicate corruption, but succeeded in antagonizing thousands of native officials, who felt deprived of the privileges granted them during Brezhnev's years of "peace and prosperity." Local Muslim party officials, because of their "persecution" by Moscow, gained popularity in the eyes of their compatriots, an element of key importance at the moment of independence.

When by 1989 Gorbachev allowed more leeway to the republics, Central Asia, traditionally indifferent to ideological symbols of Russian rule (whether Marx's writings, statues of Lenin, or Moscow-made anthems and flags), was slow to take advantage of the changed circumstances. Muslim deputies in Moscow voted in unison for every Soviet government initiative long after unanimity ceased to be the rule. Throughout the years of perestroika, Central Asian communists remained in power, and demands for national sovereignty were rarely vocal. During the March 1991 consultative referendum on the future of the USSR, Central Asia showed strong support for preserving the Union.

The resistance of local Muslim *officials* to Gorbachev's perestroika was another matter. The reform process, except for concessions to private commerce, relaxation of antireligious restrictions, and increased recognition of local cultures, was seen as an attempt to undermine local elites, or, at best, another Moscow-orchestrated campaign ill-suited to local conditions. As always, lip-service was paid to the newest Kremlin caprice, but little was ever done to implement Gorbachev's ideas.

In spring 1989, in the first semifree elections ever held in the Soviet Union, the deputies elected from Central Asia to the all-Union Supreme Soviet and the new Congress of People's Deputies turned out to be the Kremlin's most reliable supporters, voting *en bloc* for whatever the center proposed. But the price for such unquestionable support was the freeze of perestroika in Central Asia, except for the usual rhetorical compliance. Within Central Asia, local politics were more than ever determined by ethnic, regional, clan, and clique interests. Only small groups of local intellectuals endorsed the reformist struggle.

During the conservative coup attempt of August 19–21, 1991, most republican regimes in Soviet Central Asia sided with the putschists. Only Askar Akaev of Kyrgyzstan openly opposed the takeover. Even Gorbachev's close associate Nursultan Nazarbaev of Kazakhstan was slow to denounce the putsch, prudently awaiting its outcome. The preference of the majority of Central Asian party bosses for Moscow conservatives as against Moscow liberals was a key factor in their subsequent decision to seek independence from Yeltsin's Moscow, perceived as dangerous to their own rule. The demise of the Communist Party after Yeltsin's decree prohibiting its activities and confiscating its assets frightened Central Asian officialdom. The idea of national independence, previously dismissed as dangerous to officialdom's power, appeared preferable (and safer) than Yeltsin's rule. The victorious forces in Moscow were perceived as eager to promote dangerous reforms, undermine incumbent officials, and foster democratic change within the republics. At the same time, the idea of keeping looser ties with Moscow within the framework of the Commonwealth of Independent States held attractions: Russian financial assistance was not to be discarded lightly, and political ties with Moscow might be helpful for keeping Muslim fundamentalists at bay. The nomenklatura, after all, was trying to secure its position by neutralizing both the reformists on the left of the political spectrum and Muslim fundamentalists on the right.

While the Muslim party apparatus was busy jumping on the independence bandwagon, Russian officials in the republics were facing hard times. In the republics with the highest proportion of Russian settlers living in compact areas, such as Kyrgyzstan and Kazakhstan, prospects were more favorable. Thus, in Kazakhstan, Nazarbaev sought the cooperation of Russian communist officials. In Kyrgyzstan, where anticommunists came to power and old Russian *apparatchiki* lost their jobs, President Akaev courted reform-minded Russians, former officials included. But in the other three Central Asian republics the Russians fared worse: former Russian communist officials were no longer needed, while Russian reformers were feared as troublemakers. Native officials freshly draped in nationalist colors had to appear no less nationalist than their local rivals.

The demise of the Russian authority, the growth of local nationalism, the scarcity of available jobs, and blatant discrimination prompted Russian settlers to flee most rural areas, except those where they live in large numbers. The exodus of Russians and other Europeans from Central Asia (a phenomenon known as *obratnichestvo*, or return) has been under way since the 1970s and was first evident in the 1979 all-Union census data. This trend grew stronger in the 1980s, and accelerated even further in the 1990s. An exodus from Central Asian cities has also begun, and this has made life even less secure for those who remain. Russians who lack either powerful connections or valuable skills are left with few options other than remigration to mother Russia. Meanwhile, local resentment over the "garbage pail" role previously assigned to Central Asia, where all kinds of "undesirables" were exiled, ranging from kulak families in the early 1930s to "punished peoples" in the 1940s, has risen to the surface. Popular rage led to Uzbek pogroms against Meskhetian exiles from Georgia, despite the fact that the Meskhetians are Sunni Muslims and Turkic-speaking, like the Uzbeks.

After the dissolution of the Soviet Union, the exodus of outsiders accelerated, to the point of leaving some local industries stranded for lack of technical personnel. Even the strongly russified and comparatively accommodating republic of Kyrgyzstan is losing its European population.

There is at present a clear division between the republics located on the territory of the prerevolutionary General-Governorship of Turkestan, Khiva, and Bukhara, and those located on the lands of the former Steppe Region (Kazakhstan and Kyrgyzstan). The first (Uzbekistan, Tajikistan, and Turkmenistan) are governed by conservatives, harbor stronger Islamic fundamentalist elements, and keep liberal opposition under control. Political competition there is mainly between the former communists and the fundamentalists. The last two are more pro-Russian and pro-Western, and more receptive of liberal ideas. All welcome Turkish influence, but the first group is more open to Iranian and Saudi Arabian contacts as well. The struggle for the minds and hearts of Central Asian Muslims has begun.

5

The Divided Caucasus

The Caucasus, a stretch of land between the Black and Caspian seas, and to the north and south of the Caucasian mountains, is such a hodgepodge of different religions and languages that, except for the two centuries of Russian rule and the imprint of seventy years of Soviet sameness, little else unifies its various peoples. Ethnically, the population of the Caucasus may be divided into four main groups: Iranian and Turkic peoples, Slavic newcomers, and so-called Caucasian peoples, such as Armenians and Georgians, who have no ties to any other nation. Some are Muslims, others are Christians. Among Muslims there are Sunni as well as Shia groups. The Christians include Georgian, Armenian, and Russian Orthodox denominations. There are also smaller national groups, neither Christian nor Muslim, such as the Buddhist Kalmyks of the northern steppe and the Jewish Tats of the mountain slopes. Numerous languages are spoken, some, like Georgian and Armenian, having no counterparts in the rest of the world and with alphabets of their own. Even the climate varies drastically, from subtropical on the Georgian Black Sea coast to the eternal snows of the high mountains; from bare high plateaus to fertile valleys.

Until modern times, the fate of the Caucasus was closely connected with two great oriental empires—the Ottoman and the Persian. Prior to the eleventh-century Turkish conquest, it was

Byzantium that reigned on the Black Sea and it is from there that both Armenia and Georgia received the Christian faith in the fourth century. Islam arrived in the seventh century, converting the Iranian- and Turkic-speaking peoples along with some others, but failing with the Georgians and Armenians. By the seventeenth century, these two peoples, plus the partly Christian Ossetians and Abkhazians, at odds with each other, found themselves surrounded by the Muslim mountaineers in the north, Iranian-ruled Azeri Turks in the east, Iran in the south, and Ottoman Turkey in the southwest. The Georgian Black Sea coast, the only outlet for the Christian nations, was blocked, after the fifteenth-century fall of Byzantium, by the Turkish fleet, which dominated the sea. Only after the appearance of the Russian navy, and especially after the 1783 annexation of the Khanate of Crimea by the armies of Catherine the Great, was their isolation ended.

The mountain slopes of the North Caucasus, inhabited by scores of Muslim peoples, remained a barrier between Russia and the Christian part of the Transcaucasus to the south of the mountains. Turkish and Iranian influence was marginal in the north. Islam took a long time to penetrate (in some pagan areas this process was completed only between the seventeenth and nineteenth centuries), and state formation was never completed. But the mountain tribes offered determined resistance to tsarist forces (inspiring the imaginations of Pushkin, Lermontov, and Tolstoy) and provided fertile ground for Sufi brotherhoods, the most militant of the Sunni Muslim religious fraternities.

The North Caucasus can be divided into three parts. The western stretch, from the Black Sea to the Terek River, contains the Christian Ossetian wedge and was the object of the earliest Russian penetration. The central part, inhabited by the Chechens and the Ingushes, remained fiercely nationalist and militant. Finally, multiethnic Dagestan, which borders on the Caspian Sea, is a world by itself, containing ten major and sixteen minor peoples within its borders.

The Russians had maintained contacts with the Caucasus since the time of Kievan Rus, but first appeared in force only in the time of Peter the Great, who unsuccessfully attempted to extend his power along the Caspian Sea coast at the expense of Iran. After this short-lived episode, the Russians held back from the Caucasus for yet another century. With the conquest of Crimea, Russian vessels began to dominate the Black Sea, and Don Cossacks were given new lands along the Kuban River (and later along the Terek), thus pushing the Muslim population out of the valleys and deeper into the mountains.

But it was during the Napoleonic era that the conquest began in earnest. The door was opened by King Irakli II of Kakhetia (divided Georgia's main principality), who appealed for Russian protection against an anticipated Iranian invasion. While Georgians and Armenians viewed Russian protection as a lesser evil than Muslim raids, St. Petersburg saw this as an opportunity to conquer new lands and reduce the power of its southern rivals, Iran and Turkey. As Russia moved south, the Caucasian mountaineers, formerly the upper pincer of the Muslim encirclement of Georgia and Armenia, found themselves, in turn, encircled by the latter in the south and by Russia in the north, Iran and Turkey having been pushed too far south to be of serious assistance. After a half-century of "pacification," the mountaineers were overcome and subdued, and their leader Shamil captured. So by the second part of the nineteenth century, the Caucasus was firmly in Russian hands. St. Petersburg applied a divide-and-rule policy, which took advantage of tribal, religious, and ethnic conflicts among the two dozen ethnic groups of the area. Embedded local rivalries, ethnic hostilities, and religious intolerance facilitated the Russian task. The Muslim mountaineers, predominantly Sunni Muslims, were riven by tribal conflicts. The Azeri Turks, being predominantly Shia, were reluctant to aid the divided mountain tribes. The Georgians, although they appreciated the role the Armenians played as buffer between Georgia and the Muslim world, showed no Christian solidarity. The reason was that the Armenians, dispersed around Transcaucasia, were more successful in trade and commerce than their neighbors; indeed, for part of the nineteenth century they constituted the largest ethnic group in Georgia's capital city, Tbilisi, as well as in the Azeri capital, Baku. This sensitive situation made the Armenians vulnerable to local resentment. The Russian administration was only too happy to present itself as the only mediator capable of ensuring peace in the area.

In the latter half of the nineteenth century, and especially in its last quarter, the Caucasus experienced a period of growing national awareness; nationalist, revolutionary, and socialist groups multiplied. Many future Bolshevik leaders came from that region, among them Iosif Djugashvili (Joseph Stalin). Independence movements emerged in Georgia, Armenia, and Azerbaijan—movements whose appeal is being felt again today.

After the Bolshevik revolution, the three largest nations of the Transcaucasus—Armenia, Azerbaijan, and Georgia—took advantage of the weakening of the center to split from Russia. They managed to survive for about two years, until Moscow was finally able to reoccupy the region. This time, however, the conquest was presented in terms of revolutionary proletarian solidarity and a struggle against bourgeois-nationalist movements that were backed by imperialist powers. Reintegrated into the common fold, the three Transcaucasian states were first merged into a single federation, then split again in 1936, with Moscow drawing the final borders of their separate union republics. The mountain peoples of Dagestan and the North Caucasus were granted lesser status and made part of the Russian Federation (as so-called autonomous republics or regions).

This national rearrangement left many territorial issues open to future contentions. For example, the Nakhichevan Autonomous Republic, with a predominantly Azeri population, was assigned to Azerbaijan, although territorially separated from it by Armenia; Nagorno-Karabakh, with an Armenian majority, but cut off from Armenia by Azeri territory, was given the status of an autonomous region within Azerbaijan. Ossetia was split in two, its southern half made part of Georgia, while the northern half was assigned autonomous republic status within the Russian Federation. The borders of Dagestan were no less controversial, but under Stalin's iron rule the discontented parties could not venture beyond humble and discreet petitions for redress of their grievances. Not until more than half a century had passed would Gorbachev's newly granted freedoms open the gate for recriminations.

In 1988 Armenia once again laid claim to Nagorno-Karabakh in response not only to the liberalization introduced by Gorbachev but also to the appeals of Nagorno-Karabakh's Armenian majority, concerned about a shifting of the demographic balance in favor of the Azeri population. Claims and counterclaims were put forward. Azerbaijan refused to cede the region to Armenia, citing the historical unity of the Khanate of Karabakh, of which Nagornyi (Mountain) Karabakh was one component. The Armenians argued that the area had been part of ancient Armenia before the arrival of the Turkic peoples. The Azeris insisted that Karabakh Armenians were refugees from Turkish Armenia who had settled in Nagorno-Karabakh with the help of Russian authorities only in the 1830s. The dispute, which erupted in 1988, resulted in the flight of over 300,000 Armenians from Azerbaijan and of 160,000 Azeris from Armenia, an Armenian pogrom in Baku, and military intervention in that city by Soviet troops. This conflict transformed the local communist parties, brought forward patriotic national fronts, and fueled resentment against the central authorities, who were viewed as partisan, brutal, and ineffective. Moscow's bloody interventions in Tbilisi and Baku, ostensibly to restore law and order, but in reality aimed at arresting nationalist gains, only briefly slowed down the process of the unraveling of Russian power in the Transcaucasus.

Other conflicts have erupted as well, the most important among them between Georgia and Abkhazian and Ossetian separatists, the latter taking advantage of Georgia's weakening under the strain of internal political conflict.

Despite expectations, religious issues in the Caucasus have remained relatively muted. Religious fanaticism has played a small role in the Azeri-Armenian conflict. Portraits of Khomeini did appear in the streets of Baku, but this was more a protest

Table 4

Ethnic Composition of Transcaucasia (1989)

	Azerbaijan (000)	(%)	Armenia (000)	(%)	Georgia (000)	(%)
Azeris	5,805	(82.7)	85	(2.6)[a]	308	(5.7)
Armenians	391	(5.6)[a]	3084	(93.3)	437	(8.1)
Georgians	14	(0.2)	1	(—)	3,787	(70.1)
Russians	392	(5.6)[b]	52	(1.6)	341	(6.3)
Ukrainians and Belarusians	40	(0.6)	9	(0.3)	53	(1.0)
Ossetians	—		—		154	(3.0)
Abkhazians	—		—		96	(1.8)
Lezgians and Avars	215	(3.0)	—		—	
Others[c]	164	(2.3)	74	(2.2)	216	(4)[d]

Source: 1989 census.
[a]Since the 1989 census these numbers have gone down to near zero.
[b]Since 1990 the number has gone down.
[c]"Others" in Transcaucasia include 89 thousand Kurds, 28 thousand Tatars, and 35 thousand Jews.
[d]Includes 100 thousand Greeks.

against Moscow's actions than a harbinger of "holy war." While the short-lived National Front government showed a great deal of respect for Islam, Iranian-style fundamentalism finds little support in Azerbaijan. On the contrary, Iran is seen as partial to Armenia in the Karabakh conflict (presumably because it wants to discourage any Azeri designs on Iran's Azerbaijan Province). On the other side, the Catholicos of the Armenian church threw his weight behind Armenian claims in the Nagorno-Karabakh issue, but not in the name of a Christian crusade. Only in Checheno-Ingushetia, an autonomous republic in the Russian Federation, did religious forces (powerful Sufi brotherhoods) play a dominant role in pushing Chechnia onto the road to independence.

Traditional national characteristics are more important to an understanding of conflict in the Caucasus. Georgians are proud people who look down on their neighbors. Armenians are affected by a survivors' mentality. Azeris are torn between their Turkic identity and their Iranian ties: two-thirds of historic Azerbaijan is under Iranian rule.

The people of Transcaucasus are hospitable, but also attuned to personal initiative and commerce. In Russia they are regarded as shrewd traders, bribe givers, and cheats, mostly because of their prominence in Russia's food and consumer goods trade, from kolkhoz bazaars to black markets. Conversely, the Caucasians see the Russians as losers when it comes to business acumen and quality of life. Having failed to deliver on revolutionary promises and slipped from great power status, Russia cannot hold on to its "elder brother" role. The people of the Caucasus, and especially the three larger nations of the Transcaucasus, may respect Russian military might, but they no longer look to Moscow for guidance and example.

Developments in the three Transcaucasian republics since the collapse of the USSR reflect an accumulation of historical precedents and national characteristics. In Azerbaijan, the communists in power initially maintained their hold over the country by persuading the population that they were best equipped to handle the Karabakh conflict. The National Front had not yet recovered from the damage wrought by the January 1990 Soviet military intervention in Baku; it was internally divided and unprepared to assume power. As far as economic reforms were concerned, Azeri communists were as well (or as poorly) qualified as the opposition: after all, they were known as masters of private business schemes throughout the former Soviet Union.

It was the inability of the communist leadership to prevail in the Karabakh conflict that precipitated its downfall. Military defeats at the hands of better-trained Armenians became a political issue; meanwhile the National Front managed to achieve internal unity and present a challenge to the discredited communists. In May 1992 the Front came to power, which it held for barely a year. It began to build up military forces, develop close ties with Turkey, and put more distance between Baku and Moscow, but neglected to establish legitimacy by holding parliamentary elections. In June 1993 the nationalist government succumbed to a military rebellion which restored the Brezhnev-era communist leader, Heydar Aliev, to power. During all this time, Armenian forces made steady territorial gains.

In Armenia, the communists had already lost power prior to the events of August 1991, with the election of former dissident Lev Ter-Petrosian. However, the Karabakh conflict has dashed hopes for a speedy stabilization, as Armenia struggles under an Azeri economic blockade. Many Armenians emigrate abroad or to Russia, while refugees from Azerbaijan crowd the cities and exhaust local resources. Meanwhile, extreme nationalist elements cut off every avenue of peaceful resolution of the Karabakh conflict. With all this, it is hardly surprising that Armenia has been unable to rebuild from the devastating December 1988 earthquake.

Georgia, at the time of the Moscow putsch, took an ambiguous stand. Its nationalist president, Zviad Gamsakhurdia, deeply involved in fighting the opposition and punishing the rebellious Ossetians, was ready to seek accommodation with the putschists. Since Gamsakhurdia's overthrow by the military and the return to power of Eduard Shevardnadze (onetime head of the Georgian KGB, then First Secretary of the Georgian Communist Party in the early 1980s, and later USSR Foreign Minister under Gorbachev), Georgia has lost the struggle against Abkhazian separatism but has begun to emerge from its isolation. The first hope is to attract support in the struggle against separatist forces, and in the longer term to open the way to foreign aid and investments. But, since present-day Georgia, like Ukraine and Belarus, is governed by a communist apparatus whose commitment to change (despite Shevardnadze's Gorbachev-era liberal credentials) remains a question mark, the prospects for success are difficult to gauge.

6

Moldova

One of the oddities of Stalin's nationalities policy was the creation of artificial national entities for the purpose of camouflaging the outright annexation of neighboring lands. Such was the case of the Karelo-Finnish Union Republic, whose appearance in 1940 was exclusively aimed at the projected annexation of Finland. When after World War II that goal, for a variety of reasons, was finally abandoned, the republic returned to its former autonomous status within the RSFSR and the second part of its hyphenated name was dropped.

The Moldavian SSR was another artificial creation, intended to justify the annexation of a piece of Romanian territory. Essentially, Soviet Moldavia was the eastern part of Moldavia, which jointly with Wallachia forms the core of the Romanian state.

After the fifteenth-century Ottoman conquest, both Wallachia and Moldavia remained in Turkish hands, except for short periods of Polish influence. But at the beginning of the nineteenth century, as Istanbul's power slowly receded to St. Petersburg's profit, the Ottoman empire was forced to cede the eastern slice of Moldavia, east of the Prut River, to its Russian neighbor. That area, known as Bessarabia, remained in Russian hands for about a century and was not involved in the rebirth of the Romanian state. Treated as a remote province of European Russia, Bessarabia remained multiethnic: Ukrainian, Jewish, Gypsy, Tatar, and other minorities coexisted with the Moldavian (i.e., Romanian) majority. The latter, being Christian Orthodox by religion and using the Cyrillic alphabet alongside the Latin to transcribe its Romance language, remained politically unawakened and was passed over by the nationalist ferment that so strongly affected the Russian empire by the end of the nineteenth century.

After the collapse of the Romanov empire in World War I, the 1917 revolution, and the ensuing civil war, Bessarabia was incorporated into the Romanian state and remained so until 1940. But the Soviet-German Non-Aggression Pact of 1939, which divided Eastern Europe between the two expansionist powers, gave Bessarabia to Stalin. In addition to Bessarabia, Moscow demanded and received northern Bukovina, an area populated by both Moldavian Romanians and Ukrainians. This area, which prior to World War I was part of the Austro-Hungarian empire and never belonged to Russia, was incorporated into Soviet Ukraine, together with southern Bessarabia. The bulk of Bessarabia, however, was to serve as the core of a new union republic, the Moldavian SSR, which was created to erase the natural unity of eastern Moldavia with the rest of Romania.

In the 1920s Moscow had established an autonomous republic on the Soviet-Romanian border, the Moldavian ASSR, which was made part of the Ukrainian SSR. This entity, in which Moldavians were a minority, was intended to serve as the basis for the future reabsorption of Bessarabia. The fact that Friedrich Engels had once specifically cited Russian annexation of Bessarabia as a clear example of imperial expansionism posed no obstacle to Stalin's plans. Thus, when Bessarabia was recovered by Moscow in 1940, the bulk of its territory was united with part of the already existing Moldavian ASSR, whose territory was sharply reduced in Ukraine's favor and deprived of access to the Black Sea. The severing of a part of the Romanian nation from the Romanian state was accomplished. The language of Soviet Moldavians was said to be different from Romanian, and their history and culture were said to have been influenced by the Slavs since the time of Kievan Rus. This "deromanization" of Soviet

Table 5

Ethnic Composition of Moldova
(total 1989 population: 4,322,362)

Nationality group	As % of the total	Left bank (Transnistria)	Right bank (central Bessarabia)
Romanians	64	40	71
Ukrainians	14	28	10
Russians	13	26	10
Others	9[a]	6	9

Sources: 1989 census; Mikhail Guboglo, "Demography and Language in the Capitals of the Union Republics," *Journal of Soviet Nationalities*, vol. 1, no. 4, p. 21; Vladimir Socor, "Creeping Putsch in Moldova," *RFE/RL Research Reports*, vol. 1, no. 3 (January 17, 1992), p. 8.

[a]Includes 4 percent Gagauz, 2 percent Bulgarians, and under 2 percent Jews.

Moldavia remained in effect (except for the short period of Romanian occupation after the Nazi invasion of the USSR) until the mid-1980s.

After Gorbachev's accession to power and the subsequent liberalization of Soviet political life, Soviet Moldavian nationalists found themselves in a predicament: any desire for unity with Romania was strongly dampened by the unattractive character of the Ceausescu regime, which was politically repressive and economically depressed. Even after Ceausescu's fall in December 1989, the situation in Bucharest was not such as to encourage reunification. Thus Soviet Moldavian demands focused on restoring the rightful linguistic, cultural, and historic tradition of eastern Moldavia. The Cyrillic alphabet was replaced by Latin; the so-called Moldavian language was officially recognized as being a dialect of Romanian; and history texts were rewritten to represent the area's past more accurately. Moreover, Moldavia placed itself in the forefront of the independence movements by claiming real sovereignty alongside the Baltic republics. During the August 1991 putsch, Moldavia (now called Moldova, the name preferred by Moldavian nationalists) supported Yeltsin and proclaimed its independence.

Now Moldova has its own ethnic conflicts to resolve. A small Turkic-speaking Christian Orthodox ethnic group, the Gagauz, has demanded more autonomy within the republic—a move supported by Moscow, which was traditionally ready to endorse the rights of minor ethnic groups as long as they opposed the titular nationality. A potentially more lethal situation involves Slavic minorities in Transnistria (the eastern slice of Moldova located on the left bank of the Dniester River), which was never part of Romania, and where the Moldovans constitute roughly one-quarter of the total population. Since independence, the situation has grown more tense. The Russian-Ukrainian majority in Transnistria, fearful that Moldova will eventually join Romania, is determined to preserve the option of joining a Slavic entity (Ukraine?) in such a case.

There are several plausible scenarios for the future: Moldova could unite with Romania (at the risk of losing the eastern territories), enter a federation with Romania, or pursue an independent existence while maintaining close economic and political ties with both the CIS countries and Romania.

7

The Volga Basin

The six main peoples of the Volga basin—the Tatars, the Udmurts, the Bashkirs, the Mordvins, the Chuvashes, and the Maris—fell under Russian domination in the sixteenth century, when the Khanate of Kazan was conquered by Tsar Ivan the Terrible. Tatars, Bashkirs, and Chuvashes are of Turkic origin; the other three groups are Finnic. Tatars and Bashkirs are Sunni Muslims; in the course of history the others have been converted to Russian Orthodoxy. Except for the Finnic tribal region of the northern part of today's European Russia, absorbed prior to the fifteenth century, the Volga basin is the oldest colonial region of Russia and it was there that Moscow learned the ropes of colonial administration. At the outset of the sixteenth-century Russian eastward expansion, a prototype of a future colonial office, namely the *prikaz* of the Meshchera Court, was established in Moscow to take charge of alien lands. After the annexation of Kazan, the office was renamed the *prikaz* of Kazan. It operated until the time of Peter the Great, administering the conquered the khanates of Kazan and Astrakhan, and even handling Siberian affairs until the establishment of a separate Siberian *prikaz*.

Massive Russian colonization eventually made the Volga peoples a minority in most of their region. Initially, Russian peasants were brought in to populate lands granted by the tsar to Russian nobles. Later settlers were free men, looking for land and opportunity. In time, almost all the urban centers of the region became predominantly Russian. The arrival of Russian Orthodox missionaries, several revolts against Russian rule, and local participation in Russian peasant uprisings against serfdom were all symptoms of Russia's digestion of the area. It has not been a smooth process.

Of the six conquered peoples of the Volga basin, it is the two larger ones, the Tatars and the Bashkirs, that posed the most serious challenge to their conquerors. Closely connected by language, religion, and history, relatively numerous, and located on both waste and rich lands, they experienced a period of intensive national awakening toward the end of the nineteenth century. In fact, the role of the Tatars in Russian history has been tremendous. Prior to the Mongols' conquest of Kievan Rus, the Tatars had merged with the conquerors and converted them to Islam (the main horde, in Mongolia proper, as well as the one that conquered China, remained Buddhist).

For the population of Kievan Rus, the names Mongol and Tatar became interchangeable, and the thirteenth-century invasion by the Mongol "Golden Horde" became known as a Tatar invasion. To further the confusion, the Russians later gave the common name "Tatars" to nearly all the Muslim peoples they conquered.

During the 300 years of the existence of the Golden Horde—that is, between the thirteenth and sixteenth centuries—Tatar-Mongol power commanded respect among eastern Slavs. Blood ties with noble Tatar families were regarded as desirable, and in fact numerous Russian boyars allied themselves with the Tatars in this way. Even after the Golden Horde broke up into the Kazan, Astrakhan, and Crimean hordes, awe of the Tatars survived for at least another century. The rise of Moscow, which culminated in the fall of Kazan and Astrakhan in the middle of the sixteenth century, erased Tatar prestige in the Volga region. The Crimean khanate remained powerful for yet another century, before finally falling into Russian hands at the end of the eighteenth century, during the reign of Catherine the Great.

Thus, in a reversal of fortune, the Tatars turned from conquerors into the conquered. Despite their resistance to russification and unsuccessful revolts, they would play an important role in the Russian colonial expansion. Tatars served as interpreters (their Turkic language is related to the languages of Central Asia and to Azeri), intermediaries, and even agents of the Russian conqueror. Even the nineteenth-century Tatar national revival movement was torn between the desire for speedy secular Europeanization (which could only come through Russia) and Islamic tradition.

During the 1917 revolution and the ensuing civil war, both Tatars and Bashkirs attempted to create their own states. The Bashkirs were more successful. By maneuvering between the Whites and the Reds, they finally extracted generous concessions from Moscow. A bilateral treaty signed between the two parties in 1919 guaranteed the young Bashkir Republic a large degree of sovereignty, more than the union republics would be granted by successive Soviet constitutions. The treaty not only allowed the Bashkirs considerable internal autonomy but also accepted Bashkir control over their own armed forces and security apparatus. Moscow, however, failed to keep these promises and, using Russian nationals within the Bashkir Communist Party, put an end to Bashkir sovereignty. The Bashkir Republic was soon reduced to the status of an autonomous republic within the RSFSR, with little say in its own affairs.

The head of the Bashkir Revolutionary Committee, Zeki Validov, fled with his entourage to Central Asia, where he tried to help the *basmachi* resistance against Moscow, then to Istanbul. A similar fate befell the Tatar nationalists, both in Moscow and in their homeland. Sultan Galiev, a leading Tatar National-Communist and official in Narkomnats (the People's Commissariat for Nationalities), soon found himself in conflict with Stalin over the issue of class struggle in colonial areas. While Sultan Galiev argued that decolonization should take precedence, Stalin insisted on proletarian dictatorship in all corners of the country—even where the only workers were Russians and the

Table 6

Ethnic Composition of the Volga Republics of the RSFSR
(in percent, 1989)

	Tatarstan	Bashkortostan	Mari	Mordva	Udmurtia	Chuvashia
Russians	43.2	39.3	47.5	61	58.8	26.8
Ukrainians	0.9	2.5	0.7	0.7	1.0	0.5
Tatars	48.5	28.4	5.9	4.9	6.8	2.7
Bashkirs	0.5	21.9	—	—	—	—
Maris	—	2.7	43.3	—	—	—
Mordvins	0.8	1.1	0.2	32.5	0.1	1.4
Udmurts	0.7	—	0.6	—	30.9	—
Chuvashes	3.7	3.0	1.1	0.1	0.2	68.0
Others	1.7	1.1	0.7	0.8	2.2	0.6

Source: 1989 census.

"class struggle" would automatically acquire national dimensions. Obviously, what Stalin wanted was to keep control over the outlying non-Russian regions. He did so in the name of proletarian internationalism and without regard for local national aspirations, which were handily dismissed as "bourgeois."

Moscow also took pains to alter the border between the Bashkir and Kazakh republics by creating a wedge of Russian territory to separate the two entities. The effect was to make the lands of the peoples of the Volga basin appear as islands within Russian territory. In the mid-1930s, during the preparation of the so-called Stalin Constitution, Stalin rejected the Tatar request for union republic status on the grounds that Tatars could not possibly leave the Soviet Union because of their interior geographic location (technically, the Constitution allowed union republics the right to secede from the Union). Currently, both the Tatar and the Bashkir republics (Tatarstan and Bashkortostan) are again arguing for the sovereign status already won by former union republics. Culturally, the Tatar Republic is ahead of the other Turkic-speaking republics of the former USSR. Their history as intermediaries between Europe and Asia has uplifted the Tatars' educational and cultural level in a kind of compensation for their political isolation.

The story of the Chuvashes, Maris, Udmurts, and Mordvins is less well known to outsiders. Wrestled from the Kazan khanate by Moscow, they became Russia's colonies and were subjected to mass conversions, russification, and the influx of Russian settlers. The Soviet regime, by granting each of the groups the status of an autonomous republic, gave them a new lease on life. This generosity, of course, was intended to diminish the status of the more numerous and more nationalistic Tatars and Bashkirs by making them administratively equal to their smaller and weaker neighbors. It is only the current demographic weakening of the Great Russians that has finally put a stop to the further russification of these peoples. In the future, their road cannot possibly be that of independence. Federal ties with a more tolerant and democratic Moscow are their best prospects.

8

Siberia

With its over thirty million inhabitants and enormous landmass, Siberia occupies vis-à-vis European Russia a position in some ways similar to that of Canada vis-à-vis the United States. The difference is that Canada is a sovereign country, one that is itself divided into sovereign provinces that can withdraw from the federation at will. Siberia, on the other hand, is an integral part of Russia and is ruled from Moscow. Although both Siberia and Canada have indigenous minorities, Russian Siberia, unlike Canada, is dominated by a single ethnic group, the Russians. But because of their distance from the center, Siberians have different preoccupations and interests from "central Russians," to the point that many favor the establishment of an American-style federal system, which would grant Siberian "states" rights similar to those enjoyed by the states of United States.

The beginning of the Russian colonization of Siberia is connected with the Stroganov merchant family, which made its wealth in mining operations and the fur trade. At some point in the sixteenth century, their lands were comparable in size to today's Belgium. After the conquest of Kazan, fate brought the Stroganovs together with a band of adventurous Cossacks under Ataman Yermak. Eager to expand their trapping and hunting grounds to the east of the Ural Mountains, they formed an expedition, equipped and financed by the Stroganovs and manned by

Table 7

Siberia as a Part of Russia (in percent)

Territory	74.7
Population	21.8
Oil production	72.7
Gas production	88.8
Timber production	31.3

Source: *Narodnoe khoziaistvo RSFSR v tsifrakh v 1990 godu* (Moscow: Goskomstat RSFSR, 1991).

Yermak's Cossacks. Yermak brought much more than expected: not only access to untouched hunting territories, but possession of the entire "kingdom of Siberia," the southwest corner of the Siberian landmass.

This gift was presented to Tsar Ivan the Terrible, who readily added to his titles that of "Tsar of Siberia." The conquest opened the door to the further colonization of the immense and sparsely populated lands located to the north of China. (The great mystery of Siberian history was the vanishing of the Mongol presence, which left a power vacuum from the Ural Mountains to the Pacific Ocean, to be filled by Muscovite Russia.) During the next seventy years, explorers, hunters, Cossacks, and merchants moved eastward, using waterways in the summer and snow tracks in the winter, and building little wooden forts and trading outposts along the way. Russian administration followed, stationing soldiers for protection and clerks for the collection of taxes, including a head tax in furs from the local natives. The two main directions of Russian colonial expansion were eastward to the Pacific Ocean, stopping at the borders of Chinese power, and northward to the Arctic, where only nature posed an obstacle. By the end of the nineteenth century the Trans-Siberian railroad connected Moscow with Russian ports on the Pacific Ocean.

Basically, Siberia can be divided into three parts: the Far East, near the borders of China, Korea, and Japan (after the civil war of 1918–20, an "independent republic" was set up there); central

Siberia, comprising the bulk of Siberian territory; and western Siberia, which lies east of the Urals and to the north of the Kazakh lands. Within each north-south slice of Siberian territory, there are autonomous republics and regions, named after the local indigenous populations. Without exception, Russians outnumber the indigenous group in each of these units, their majorities ranging from overwhelming to slight. These national units were established after the revolution, but their recognition rarely extended beyond a right to preserve folkloric traditions, and left governance, the economy, and the ecology under the Kremlin's control.

Siberia also served as a depository for all kinds of deportees, ranging from common criminals to political dissenters. The practice of removing dangerous people (or persons so perceived) to Siberia started at the time of its conquest, became common in the nineteenth century, and reached its high point during Stalin's purges. At worst these prisoners were put to hard labor in mines; at best they were allowed to live freely in specifically assigned areas while periodically reporting to police authorities. Concentration camps—the so-called "gulags"—were a Soviet innovation, since the existing penal installations could not possibly handle the millions of inmates. Major Siberian construction projects, ranging from the Bratsk Hydroelectric Station to the city of Komsomolsk, were built by prisoners working under subhuman conditions. As a result, some regions of Siberia are better known for their gulags than anything else. After Stalin's death, and especially after Khrushchev's denunciation of Stalin in 1956, the numbers of inmates dwindled. The last political prisoners were freed by Gorbachev. Still, given the large number of common criminals incarcerated in the USSR, some camps continued to operate under conditions that would shock a Westerner.

However, the image of Siberia as a place of camps, eternal frost, and endless tundra is incomplete. Rich in oil, gas, and minerals, containing large industrial cities and cultural centers, Siberia remains a land of great potential. True, there are areas affected by air and water pollution, and dying forests, but there are also unspoiled stretches of land, natural beauty, and rich fauna. To these essential assets one should add the strong independence of the Siberian spirit, born of the absence of serfdom, the comfortable distance from autocratic Moscow and St. Petersburg, and a Texan-type consciousness of living in an abundant world of vast scale. In recent years, Siberian miners have been in the forefront of reform and the independent trade union movement, and they threw their support to Yeltsin during the aborted putsch. Likewise, some Siberian native peoples, such as the Sakha (Yakuts), whose autonomous republic is enormous in size and rich in a wide range of mineral resources, have become conscious of the opportunity to have a say about the disposal of these riches. In northwestern Siberia, along the Irtysh River, the tiny Mansi tribe wants a "divorce" from its Khant partner, with whom it shares an autonomous republic. On the Mongolian border, Tannu-Tuva, annexed by Stalin during World War II, is experiencing a rebirth of nationalist feeling. These republics, along with Buryatia, are even presenting territorial claims to neighboring Russian regions, claims that up until now are being peacefully expressed. In the Far East reliance on Moscow is stronger: hope for Japanese investments is mitigated by the fear of Japanese economic power and the necessity of returning the southern Kurile Islands to Tokyo.

Whatever the future portends, Siberia with its riches will play a key role in redirecting Russia's path.

Part 2

Minorities

1

The "Punished Peoples"

In 1937 the Koreans who lived in the Soviet Far East, north of the Korean border, were shipped to Central Asia. This step, motivated by Moscow's distrust of all "yellow Asians" on the eve of Soviet-Japanese border clashes, was the first of its kind for the regime: the wholesale repression of a group of the population on the basis not of social but rather national origin.

The tragic story of the "punished peoples" of the USSR is one with almost no parallel in history, exceeded only by the Holocaust of the Jews under Nazi Germany and the massacre of Armenians living in the Ottoman empire at the time of World War I. True, unlike the Jews or the Armenians, the punished peoples of the USSR were not slaughtered, but deported, though many died in transit. Those who survived were allowed to rebuild their lives in exile. But none were spared deportation, not even soldiers who fought in the ranks of the Red Army against the Nazis. By contrast, the mass deportations from territories annexed by the USSR as a result of the Soviet-German Non-Aggression Pact were essentially based on distrust of people's class or political background.

Eight separate peoples were affected by wartime deportations: Volga Germans, Crimean Tatars, Chechens, Ingushes, Karachai, Balkars, Kalmyks, and Meskhetian Turks. In addition, two tiny minority populations, the Kurds living in the Caucasus and the Finns of Ingermanland (Petersburg), shared the fate of other punished peoples, although neither they nor the Meskhetians were accused—as all the others were—of collaboration with the Germans. Around three-quarters of a million people were exiled to Kazakhstan, Central Asia, or Siberia. The number does not seem too great in comparison with the total of Stalin's deportees; what is striking is that in each case a national group was affected in its entirety. Given the fact that persons of other nationalities also collaborated with the German occupiers, first of all the Russians themselves, the collective punishment administered to selected nations must have had some other purpose as well.

The Volga Germans (discussed in more detail in chapter 3, below) were obviously singled out as a potential "fifth column" and their deportation had a preventive character. It took place in 1941, before the German advance to Stalingrad, and so can be attributed to war hysteria of the moment. In the United States similar measures were taken against Japanese-Americans.

The Kalmyks, a remnant of a formidable nomad horde that had been pushed westward first by the Mongols, then by the Kazakhs and the Bashkirs, and finally settled to the west of the Volga River at the borders of the Caucasus, were also among the punished. Annexed by Russia in the sixteenth century, the Kalmyks were allowed to live according to their own Buddhist tradition. During the civil war in Russia, they showed more sympathy for the Whites, and later suffered from collectivization and other measures to end their nomadic ways. Disillusioned with the Soviet regime, some Kalmyks made the mistake of betting on a German victory at Stalingrad, thus bringing Stalin's wrath against their entire nation. Still, the Kalmyks were rather lucky. In 1956 they were "forgiven" (rehabilitated) and allowed to return home. Their autonomous republic was reestablished (after some minor territorial losses). However, the Kalmyks had to wait for Gorbachev's liberalization to obtain religious freedom. Their current aspirations are cultural and economic rather than separat-

Table 8

Punished Peoples
National Groups Deported in Their Quasi-Totality (in 000)

Deported nation	1939 census	Number of deaths during the first 5 years of exile	In exile by January 1, 1953	1989 census
Koreans[a]	182	40[b]	n.d	439
Germans[c]	1,424	300	1,225	2,039
Chechens	408	100[d]	317	957
Ingushes	92	23[d]	83	237
Karachai	76	19[d]	63	156
Balkars	43	11[e]	33	85
Crimean Tatars	191	42–88[f]	165	272
Meskhetian Turks	115	15	49	208
Kalmyks	93	16[g]	81	174
Kurds	80	n.d.	9	153

Source: Helsinki Watch, *"Punished Peoples" of the Soviet Union, The Continuing Legacy of Stalin's Deportations* (September 1991), corrected with estimates by Sidney Heitman and Viktor Kozlov; 1953 data: M. P. Polian, "Spetskontinent," in: *Migratsiia naseleniia* (Moscow: Institute of Employment Problems, Russian Academy of Sciences, 1992).

[a]The Koreans were deported in 1937. All the others were deported during World War II.

[b]Korean deaths during the first year of exile.

[c]According to Sidney Heitman, 600,000 Germans were deported from the Volga German Autonomous Republic and elsewhere in 1941, and another 250,000 from the western part of the USSR after the end of the war. According to M. P. Polian, 447,000 Germans were deported in 1941 from the Volga German republic and neighboring regions and 502,700 from elsewhere; 120,000 more German repatriates from Germany and Austria were added by 1949.

[d]Chechen, Ingush, Karachai, and Balkar deaths were officially estimated at 24.7 percent of all the deportees of the four nationalities combined.

[e]Balkar numbers include 3,500 deaths in transit.

[f]Crimean Tatar numbers include 7,900 deaths in transit. The first figure is an official estimate; the second is from a Crimean Tatar source.

[g]The Kalmyk figure includes 1,200 deaths in transit.

ist. The Kalmyk Republic attracted world attention in 1990, but this was because of an AIDS epidemic in the maternity ward in Elista (the Kalmyk capital), caused by contaminated needles.

The deported mountain peoples of the Caucasus (Chechens, Ingushes, Karachai, and Balkars) are all Sunni Muslims, with a history of fighting Russian conquest in the nineteenth century. Evidently they were victims of Stalin's distrust of Georgia's Muslim neighbors.

After the Russian conquest, many Caucasian mountaineers fled to the Ottoman empire (King Hussein of Jordan's personal guard is still made up of Circassians, descendants of refugees from the Caucasus). But after decades of revolts, the shock of conquest dissipated, and the tsarist authorities managed to pacify the region. The Russian cavalry even enrolled special "savage" units made up exclusively of Caucasian Muslims. During the revolution, these units found themselves mostly on the side of the Whites. Nevertheless, at the outset of the Soviet regime, the mountaineers clearly benefited from the new Soviet nationalities policy, and received their own national-territorial units endowed with various degrees of autonomy (as either autonomous republics or autonomous regions within the RSFSR). Later, as victims of Stalin's paranoia, they were accused, along with the Kalmyks, of aiding the German troops entering the North Caucasus. Deported under harsh conditions, they were rehabilitated some twelve years later and allowed to return home. Their old national-territorial units were restored, albeit within somewhat altered borders. Symbolic of the shifting Soviet policies was Moscow's official attitude toward Shamil, the principal Caucasian leader who fought the nineteenth-century Russian conquest. After the October Revolution he was depicted as an anticolonialist fighter; during the Stalin era he was denounced as a British and Turkish agent; after Stalin's death Shamil was rehabilitated as heroic blunderer who had been unable to comprehend the benefit of Russian conquest.

After their return, the Caucasian mountaineers managed to reestablish their own way of life (the Chechens forcefully expelled those who occupied their homes, if the latter were unfortunate enough to be around at the time of their return).

One important institution that survived Soviet repression is the Sufi brotherhoods, which in the Chechen region became the power behind the facade of Soviet administration. These brotherhoods were so tightknit that they managed to penetrate the local

KGB, and not the contrary. Today the brotherhoods are more influential than ever, especially among the Chechens, who became the first among autonomous republics to proclaim independence, both from the former USSR and from the Russian Federation.

At present, the situation in the Chechen region is complex: the Ingush part of what was the Checheno-Ingush Autonomous Republic reverted to its former separate status of the 1920s. The Chechen Republic itself, led by General Djokhar Dudaev, remains in a state of uneasy truce with Russia, which for the time being has refrained from seeking to bring the stray republic back into its fold. The situation within the republic is also very touchy: internal dissensions flourish, and relations with the Russian minority are tense, especially with the Terek Cossacks. Moreover, plans for the reestablishment of a Mountain Republic, which existed for a short while in 1920, uniting all the Muslim lands of the North Caucasus, are being widely discussed. Such an entity could pose a serious threat to the Russian presence in the area and is being opposed by Moscow.

The most difficult case among the punished peoples is that of the Crimean Tatars. Originally a splinter of the Mongol-Tatar Golden Horde, they remained powerful for at least a century after the fall of Kazan and Astrakhan. As Crimea slowly lost its former strength, it turned to Istanbul for protection, but with the weakening of the Ottoman empire, that aid did not suffice. Crimea finally fell into Russian hands during the reign of Catherine the Great. For Crimean Tatars, this fall was a traumatic experience, a transition from power to powerlessness. The Russians, for their part, not only looked down on the "uncivilized" Tatars, but saw them as the last remnant of the Mongol horde that invaded Kievan Rus in the thirteenth century, bringing terror and desolation. Russian officials were attentive to the Byzantine heritage of the area, but saw little need of preserving the Muslim cultural heritage, historical sites, and religious monuments. Despite massive Russian colonization, the Crimean Tatars experienced a strong intellectual awakening in the nineteenth century, spurred by such men as Ismail Gaspirali, who attempted to combine local tradition with European culture as transmitted through Russia.

After the victory of the Bolsheviks, a Crimean Tatar Autonomous Republic was created as part of the RSFSR. The Tatars constituted about one-quarter of the total population in their own republic and during the Soviet period they went through the same experience as other peoples of the USSR, with their national culture reduced to folkloric manifestations. However, the very existence of a national-territorial unit with its own government apparatus, even if powerless, gave the Tatars a sense of national continuity. This was shattered during World War II, after Soviet forces drove the German Army out of Crimea. Crimean Tatars were collectively accused of collaboration and deported to Central Asia, alongside other punished peoples. Despite "rehabilitation" in the Khrushchev era, the Crimean Tatars were refused repatriation to their native land. Indeed, to mark the three-hundredth anniversary of the "union of Ukraine with Russia," Khrushchev gave Crimea to Ukraine as an anniversary "gift," a unique event in the history of interethnic relations. Moscow claimed that the Tatars' place in Crimea had already been taken by Russian and Ukrainian settlers, who could not be dislodged, and that, after all, the Crimean Tatars who now resided in Uzbekistan were living amid Turkic-speaking people of similar culture and origin. Those Crimean Tatars who tried to return home on their own were given a hard time by local authorities, even when they managed to buy back their own houses and find employment.

By 1990 the Tatars were no longer officially prevented from returning to Crimea, and approximately fifty thousand of them managed to settle on the peninsula. But the final disposition of the matter is still pending, and all its related problems—ranging from restoration of autonomy to restitution of confiscated properties—are not only still unresolved, but further complicated by Ukrainian independence.

The case of the Meskhetian Turks is different from that of other punished peoples. The smallest among the deported groups, the Meskhetians were living in Georgia and not in the Russian Republic, and enjoyed no special territorial autonomy. They were deported from Georgia to Uzbekistan on Stalin's orders (and with the blessing of Georgian authorities). Subsequently, the Meskhetians were not accepted back into Georgia. Those who left the area of forced settlement and returned to the Caucasus stopped in Azerbaijan, where they remain. The Meskhetians had the recent misfortune of suffering a pogrom at the hands of the Uzbeks, among whom they dwelled in exile and who resented their economic success.

The futures of the punished peoples promise to be more diverse than their fate under Stalin: for the Germans, emigration to a unified Germany, a country their ancestors left more than two centuries ago; for the Crimean Tatars, restoration of their national-territorial autonomy, although probably only in the eastern corner of the peninsula; for all the others, the experience of deportation and exile survives in hellish images of a bygone national history, feeding a justified mistrust of Moscow.

2

The Jews

In historical terms, Russian Jewry is a recent phenomenon, dating only from the end of the eighteenth century. Prior to that time, no Jews were allowed to live in Russia. The few who did had to convert to Russian Orthodoxy. The most famous among them, Piotr Shafirov, was an adviser to Peter the Great in the early 1700s.

Kievan Rus prior to the Mongol invasion had its own encounter with Judaism, when the ruling class of its southeastern neighbors, the Khazars, espoused the Jewish faith. But by the time of the thirteenth-century Mongol invasion, the Khazars had vanished from the scene. The next "meeting" between the Russians and the Jews took place in the middle of the sixteenth century, when Russian troops took the town of Polotsk from the Poles and found within it a number of Jewish inhabitants. On the tsar's orders, those Jews who refused to convert were drowned in the river. Afterward, during the numerous Polish-Muscovite negotiations, the Russians consistently refused to allow Jewish merchants from Poland the right to trade in Muscovy—this despite the intercession of Polish kings on behalf of the Jews.

By contrast, the Polish-Lithuanian state was lenient to Jews, who had begun fleeing eastward across Europe at the time of the Spanish Inquisition. The Jewish population of the Polish-Lithuanian Commonwealth, despite latent popular anti-Semitism, benefited from the protection of Polish kings and the tolerance of the Polish nobility, with whom the Jews had developed mutually beneficial business relations. Still, the Jews lived apart from the rest of the population, confined to their "shtetls" (Jewish townships), squeezed between noblemen's estates and peasant villages.

As a result of the three partitions of Poland at the end of the eighteenth century, this Jewish population found itself split among Austro-Hungary, Prussia, and Russia. The latter became the reluctant host to the majority of Polish-Lithuanian Jewry. After going through several policy shifts, St. Petersburg finally settled (by the end of the nineteenth century) on a specific policy toward the over five million Jews residing within the confines of the Romanov empire.

The key to that policy was the creation of the so-called "pale of settlement" within the former Polish-Lithuanian territories and the areas annexed from the Crimean Tatars. Except for a few large cities that required special permits, Jews were authorized to reside only within the borders of the pale. Outside of that area, and particularly in Moscow and St. Petersburg, Jewish settlement was limited to certain social classes: rich merchants and important industrialists, individuals with university diplomas, craftsmen with rare skills, and prostitutes. Educational institutions were given admission quotas for Jewish applicants, ranging from a maximum of 10 percent within the pale to the usual 3 percent in the large cities (quotas did not apply to private institutions). Jews were banned from the civil service and the officer corps, prohibited to own land in most areas, and even restricted in trade outside the pale and export trade. Worse, public discontent was often conveniently channeled into anti-Jewish pogroms, spurred by accusations of "ritual murder" leveled against the Jews as recently as the early twentieth century.

Confined to the pale and treated as second-rate subjects of the empire, the Jews lived mostly in small towns, socially and culturally segregated not only by their Christian neighbors but also by their own resistance to outside influence. The neighbors of the

Jews were Ukrainian and Belarusian peasants, Polish and Russian landowners, Russian bureaucrats and policemen, all of whom represented the "outside world."

By the end of the nineteenth century, taking advantage of the opportunities of the industrial boom of the Russian empire, Jews began to abandon their centuries-old seclusion. Some moved upward on the social ladder, gaining acceptance from the Russian middle class and intellectuals; others migrated to the United States in search of a better life; still others were attracted by revolutionary visions and joined a variety of socialist causes. Many were stirred by the emerging Zionist ideal of return to the land of Israel.

After the October Revolution, prosperous Jews emigrated, Zionists were silenced, and national equality under the new Soviet regime became the only hope. It meant the end of the pale and of admission quotas, the opening of all careers, and an opportunity to build a new society based on social justice and ethnic tolerance. The number of Jews in high positions became disproportionately large wherever the Jewish intelligentsia replaced the part of the Russian intelligentsia that was unwilling to cooperate with the new regime. It was a time of Jewish commissars in leather jackets, penalties for anti-Semitism, movement of Jews from the shtetls to large cities, and entry of Jews into universities, party posts, the government, the army, and the security apparatus.

The honeymoon with the Soviet regime was short-lived. Stalin's vision of "socialism in one country" had little room for internationally minded Jewish activists; fresh Russian cadres were being groomed in "workers' faculties"; and most of all, the argumentative disposition of Jewish intellectuals did not fit well with Stalin's demand for total conformity. During the purges of the 1930s, most Jewish communists with a revolutionary past were eliminated; the few who remained were shunted aside. By the end of the 1930s, Russian Jewry found itself in a confused situation—useful for its technical prowess, but no longer needed in the command-control apparatus.

The Nazi attack on the USSR in 1941 enhanced the status of

Soviet Jews, whose reliability in the war against fascism was a recognized fact. But by the end of the war, and especially after the beginning of the Cold War, the Jews had played out their usefulness for the regime and were increasingly singled out as unreliable, especially in view of their family connections abroad and their presumed allegiance to Israel. A distinction was made between antipatriotic "cosmopolitan tendencies" ascribed to Jews and the "true internationalism" said to characterize the new Soviet man. Nazi extermination of Soviet Jews was not a subject for discussion: Soviet citizens of all nationalities were said to have suffered equally during the war. In 1952, shortly before his death, Stalin was ready to add the Jews to his list of "punished peoples" by deporting them wholesale to Birobijan, the small Jewish autonomous region on the Chinese border that was artificially created to compete with the attraction of the Jewish national home in Palestine. Although after Stalin's death this idea was buried together with the anticosmopolitan campaign, the Jews found new walls erected in front of them: admission quotas in universities, hiring barriers, frozen promotions, greater than average travel difficulties, prohibition of Hebrew instruction, cultural restrictions, and tolerance of open anti-Semitism. This situation, which lasted until the Gorbachev years, prompted a new wave of Jewish emigration.

During the 1970s, a quarter of a million of Soviet Jews emigrated abroad, mostly to the United States, partly to Israel. The exodus, the first of its kind from the USSR since civil war days, was the combined result of U.S. pressure and Soviet aspirations for better trade relations with the United States. Soviet anti-Semitism played its role as well: departing Jews were vacating jobs and apartments desired by their neighbors, and removing their own undesirable presence as well. The war in Afghanistan and worsening U.S.-Soviet relations stopped the exodus until the late 1980s, when it was resumed on a much larger scale.

The present-day situation of Russian Jewry is very complex, a paradoxical mixture of assimilation and alienation. The signs of assimilation include the replacement of Yiddish by Russian as the principal "mother tongue" for the great majority of Russian

Table 9

Jewish Population (1897–1993)

Year	Number (000)	Remarks
1897	5,063	Within pre–World War I borders, based on native language
1926	2,672[a]	71.9% show Yiddish as native language
1937	2,715	Data only recently published
1939	3,029	
1941	5,000	Approximate figure; includes Jews in annexed areas
1959	2,268	Shows losses during World War II
1970	2,151	
1979	1,811[b]	14.2% show Yiddish as native language
1989	1,449	
1993	1,100[c]	

Sources: Russian and USSR censuses. For 1993: Shimon Chertok, "Alia: vchera, segodnia, zavtra," *Novoe Russkoe Slovo* (New York), March 15, 1993, quoting estimates from the Department of Demography, Hebrew University of Jerusalem.

[a]1,470 in Ukraine; 363 in Belorussia.

[b]Including RSFSR—701; Ukraine—634; Belorussia—135; Moldavia—80; Lithuania—15; Latvia—28; Estonia—5; Azerbaijan—35; Georgia—28; Uzbekistan—100; Tajikistan—15.

[c]Russian Federation—450; Ukraine—400; Belarus—60; Moldova—30; Azerbaijan, Georgia, Kazakhstan, and Latvia—15 each; Estonia—3; Turkmenistan—1.5; Armenia—0.5; Lithuania—n.d.

Jews, large-scale intermarriage (over three-quarters of Jewish marriages are with non-Jewish partners), and active participation in political reform movements (both in Russia and in other republics). The main indicator of alienation is the panicky exodus, motivated by the fear of vocal anti-Semitism as well as by continuous economic hardships.

Anti-Jewish restrictions and quotas have been lifted, but the new freedom enjoyed by Soviet society has also allowed the open expression of anti-Jewish sentiments. Thus Jews are blamed

Table 10

Jewish Population in the Capitals of Union Republics (1989)

Capital	Number	% of total population
Moscow	173,825	2.0
Kiev	100,427	3.9
Minsk	39,029	2.5
Vilnius	9,109	1.6
Riga	18,812	2.1
Tallinn	3,620	0.8
Kishinev	35,518	5.4
Erevan	550	—
Baku	20,132	1.7
Tbilisi	6,828	0.5
Alma-Ata	7,615	0.7
Dushanbe	12,031	2.0
Tashkent	43,056	2.1

Source: Mikhail Guboglo, "Demography and Language in the Capitals of the Union Republics," *Journal of Soviet Nationalities,* vol. 1, no. 4 (Winter 1990–91).

Notes: No data for Ashkhabad or Bishkek. Among Jews in Dushanbe, 4,165 were Bukharan Jews.

for supporting the revolution in the first place and participating in the subsequent terror, as well as for such "sins" as "eating all the butter," "polluting the Russian language," and "destroying old Moscow in the 1930s." The fact that since the 1930s Soviet Jews, with rare exceptions, have been totally excluded from power seems to have been forgotten.

The exact number of Soviet Jews is hard to establish. The 1989 census set the figure at 1,449,000, down from 1,811,000 in 1979; but if half-Jews and undeclared Jews are accounted for, the total may be doubled. Jewish losses during World War II and the German occupation are also difficult to determine: on the eve of the German invasion roughly five million Jews resided in the USSR, including areas annexed by Moscow in 1939–40. Prior to the mass emigration to United States and Israel, some left the Soviet Union for Poland in 1945–46 and in 1956. Over two million must have perished during the Nazi occupation.

According to the 1989 census, the Russian Republic housed over half of Soviet Jews, Ukraine a third, the Baltic republics about 40,000 (mostly postwar émigrés), and the Muslim republics over 100,000. Only about 7,000 Jews live in Birobijan (less than 5 percent of its population). Among non-Ashkenazi (or non-European) Jews are the Mountain Jews (Tats) of the Caucasus, the Georgian Jews, and the Bukharan Jews of Central Asia (making up less than 5 percent of the total Jewish population).

Jewish organizations (Zionist included) have reemerged in recent years, but attract only a small percentage of the Jewish population. The typical Soviet Jew is Russian-speaking, middle-class with a college education, nonreligious, and politically cynical.

Three events have shaped the current position of Russian Jewry: the closing of U.S. doors to most Jewish immigrants, who are no longer regarded as refugees from Soviet oppression; absorption difficulties in Israel (economic hardships, as well as the war in the Persian Gulf and the Palestinian troubles); and finally, new opportunities in Russia after the failure of the conservative putsch in August 1991.

The process of democratization in Russia and in other republics of the former Soviet Union has given hope of a more promising future for the remaining Jewish population. Jews are numerous in the democratic movements (one of the three young men who fell defending the "White House" in August 1991 was a Jew). In the newly independent Baltic states, national governments are doing their utmost to be fair with the small Jewish minorities on their soil; they are far more ambivalent about their large Russian (or Polish) minorities. While Jewish emigration will undoubtedly continue, the former Soviet republics will probably retain some Jewish population unless reactionary forces gain ground, provoking a new exodus.

3

The Germans

The Germans first appeared in seventeenth-century Russia as traders, mercenaries, and craftsmen. Although confined to the *Nemetskaia sloboda* (German quarter) in Moscow, they soon became carriers of Western influence, replacing the more familiar but (in Russian eyes) less prestigious Poles. Under Peter the Great, Germans were invited to staff the first Russian academic institutions, but the total number of Germans in the country remained small. It was only after Peter's conquest of Estonia and northern Latvia, areas with a large German noble class, that the German numerical presence became significant.

German influence at the Russian Court grew throughout the eighteenth century, reaching its highest point with the marriage of the future Tsar Peter III to a princess of Anhalt-Zerbst, the future Catherine II of Russia. After coming to power by eliminating her husband, Catherine further enhanced the already favorable position enjoyed by the Germans in Russia. She opened the door for foreign settlers ("except Jews") to populate the banks of the lower Volga, granting them financial assistance and legal protection. The newcomers, preponderantly Germans, managed to establish prosperous agricultural colonies, which preserved the German way of life and language. Mostly Protestant and apolitical, they adapted well and prospered, for which they were envied by their Russian neighbors.

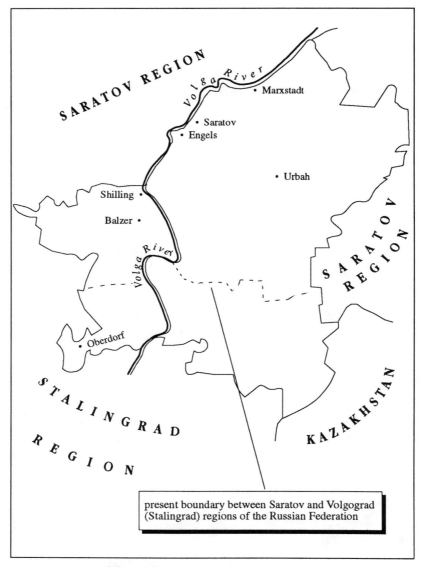

present boundary between Saratov and Volgograd (Stalingrad) regions of the Russian Federation

The Volga-German Autonomous Republic in Its 1940 Borders

During the nineteenth century, Russian Germans grew in numbers and prosperity. Respected and favored by the Court, these Volga settlers, Baltic noblemen, Russified aristocrats, and urban craftsmen found Russia most hospitable. Even after the October Revolution, those Germans who remained within the confines of the Soviet state retained their prestige, though now as compatriots of Marx and Engels and potential sowers of a future revolution in Germany. To ensure a proper status for the Germans, a Volga German Autonomous Republic was created (for Stalin, territory was a prerequisite of status). Even in the wake of collectivization, which so devastated agricultural communities throughout the USSR, Volga Germans managed to maintain a much higher standard of living than their Russian neighbors.

The demise of Soviet Germans took place in three stages:

1. Pursuant to the Soviet-German Non-Aggression Pact of August 1939, by which Hitler and Stalin divided Eastern Europe between them, ethnic Germans remaining in the Baltic republics conceded by Berlin to Moscow were repatriated to the German Reich.
2. After Germany attacked the USSR, the Volga German Autonomous Republic was abolished and its German inhabitants deported to Kazakhstan.
3. Simultaneously, Germans living outside of the Volga German Republic were deported as well, including families of Germans serving in the Red Army.

Thus when Moscow emerged victorious after World War II, the Germans were no longer a favored, but a persecuted, minority. The almost two-million-strong German population of the USSR had by then been dispersed across Kazakhstan (over half) and the rest of Central Asia, with smaller numbers in Siberia and elsewhere. Yet even as third-rate citizens—dominated both by the titular nationality of the host republic and by the Russians, and subjected to constant discrimination—Germans managed to emerge as the key economic actors in the areas of German con-

Table 11

Germans in the Former USSR (population in thousands)

	1953	1989
Total	1,225	2,037
Including		
in the RSFSR	771	845
in Kazakhstan	449	958
in Kyrgyzstan	16	101
in the rest of Central Asia	38	77
in Ukraine and Belorussia	1	41
in the 3 Baltic republics	—	9
in the Transcaucasus	—	2
in Moldavia	—	7

Source: 1953 data: M. P. Polian, "Spetskontinent," in *Migratsiia naseleniia* (Moscow: Institute of Employment Problems, Russian Academy of Sciences, 1992); 1989 data: *Etnopolis*, 1992, no. 2 (February), pp. 155–56.

centration. When, after Stalin's death, German delegates petitioned Moscow for the right to return to their former homes, they were told that they were indispensable in Kazakhstan and Central Asia and should remain there (a compliment of a sort).

Thus Soviet Germans found themselves in an uncomfortable predicament: they were permanently confined to the Asian part of the USSR, with no political future and a restricted cultural life. Their only asset was the possibility of economic betterment through their own hard work. And in fact some Germans did achieve "upward mobility" through promotion to managerial status. But the bulk of Germans remained in subordinate jobs under Russian or Muslim bosses.

It was the beginning of Jewish emigration in the 1970s that finally opened the door for Soviet Germans. Following the Jewish example, they sought the right to emigrate and thus encountered similar obstacles. But with growing West German support and pressure (including financial incentives offered by Bonn to Moscow), mass emigration began. Today, a unified Germany admits thousands of German immigrants every month, the great grandsons and -daughters of German émigrés of two centuries ago, who may know little about their ancestral homeland.

Although several alternatives to German emigration have been envisaged, none of them is very attractive for would-be emigrants.

1. The possibility of reestablishing the old German autonomy on the Volga is an idea that had a lot more appeal twenty or thirty years ago than it has in the 1990s. Moreover, the local Russian population, which has occupied the old German farms and managed to run them down over the past decades, would oppose such a reversal of fortune.
2. Relocation to the Baltic states, where there has been a German presence for centuries, has served mainly as a short-term solution for Soviet Germans who moved from Central Asia and Kazakhstan to Latvia only as a waystation on the road to Germany.
3. To open the Kaliningrad region (formerly Königsberg) for massive settlement by Germans from the Asian republics with the help of German financing and investments and creation of a special free-trade zone. The question is whether Volga Germans could be lured to move to Kaliningrad instead of to Germany proper, whether the local Russian settlers would cooperate, and whether German capital could in fact be attracted.

What is most likely is that Germans will accelerate their mass exodus from their places of exile in Central Asia and Kazakhstan and will seek destinations outside the former USSR. Thus the long history of the Germans in the Russian empire is coming to a close.

4

Minorities Within the Republics

The former union republics of the USSR are themselves multi-ethnic: they harbor minorities within their borders, not least among them Russians. In some cases, these "non-titular" nationalities are nations that occupy their own historic homelands, but were considered too small in size to qualify for union-republic status. In other cases, these are large nations, but they are densely intermingled with the "titular" nationality, or encircled by the latter's territory, preventing a clear-cut separation between the two. During Stalin's time, such "minority" nations, depending on their size and demographic situation, were sometimes granted a lesser national-territorial status as autonomous republics, autonomous regions, or national districts (in descending order of rank). This was not done in *matrëshka*-doll fashion, with units of decreasing size located within each other; rather, each nationality within a union republic had (or lacked) its own territorial status. The largest of all the union republics, the RSFSR (the Russian Federation), housed a score of autonomous republics, regions, and districts, while some other union republics contained none.

There are also many national minorities that occupy extensive territory within a republic but lack national-territorial autonomy, mostly because they have spilled over from a neighboring republic, or because old borders have been altered. This is the case of the Poles in Lithuania, the Tajiks in Uzbekistan, and the Uzbeks in Kyrgyzstan, to name just a few examples.

Of all the former republics, it is Georgia that now has the most complex problem, with three national-territorial autonomies within its borders. Keeping Georgian territory undivided is a high priority for Tbilisi, and the Kremlin realized very well that playing on Abkhazian, Ossetian, and Ajar separatism was a way to keep Georgia off balance. The Abkhazians, who are only about 20 percent of the population within their own autonomous republic (with Georgians accounting for roughly 60 percent, and Russians and others for the rest), have reasserted their ethnic and linguistic separateness. Under Gorbachev, the Kremlin, eager to undermine the aspirations of the Georgian national-independence movement, initially encouraged the Abkhazians in another variation of the old divide-and-rule game. A second group, the Ossetians, are divided between two territorial entities: one, within the Russian Federation, enjoys autonomous republic status, while the other, to the south, is an autonomous region within Georgia. Here the problem is not demography but geopolitics, for the southern Ossetian territory slices through historically Georgian lands. Its separation would wreak havoc with Georgia's territorial integrity, communications, and economy. The third case, the Ajar Autonomous Republic, is totally different, for the Ajars are ethnic Georgians, distinguished only by their religion—Islam.

In Uzbekistan there is only one non-Uzbek territorial subunit, the Kara-Kalpak Autonomous Republic. The Kara-Kalpaks, although they are linguistically and culturally closer to the Kazakhs than to the Uzbeks, have old ties with the Khanate of Khiva, historically an Uzbek-dominated entity. Nevertheless, the future of Kara-Kalpakia is bleak not because of national confrontation with the Uzbeks, but because of virtually total ecological devastation: their key natural resource, the Aral Sea, is dying.

The Armenians of the Nagorno-Karabakh Autonomous Region of Azerbaijan represent the most difficult case of Soviet interethnic relations. Territorially encircled by Azerbaijan, historically part of the Azeri Khanate of Karabakh, but demographically predominantly Armenian, the region is a powder keg. Armenian connections with the area date from antiquity, but were interrupted for centuries. Then in the early nineteenth century there was a mass migration of Armenians into Karabakh from the neighboring Armenian provinces of the Ottoman empire. Since the Russian civil war of 1918–20, the Armenians have tried several times to unite the High Karabakh to Armenia proper, only to see their efforts blocked by the Turks, the Russians, or the Azeris. In 1988 the Armenians attempted unification once again, with tragic consequences: anti-Armenian pogroms in Azerbaijan, the exodus of all Azeris from Armenia and of all Armenians from Azerbaijan proper, a recurrent civil war in and around Nagorno-Karabakh, and an excessive preoccupation with the issue on the part of both the Azeris and the Armenians, with a Yugoslav scenario very much in the making.

The Poles of Vilnius are another difficult case. The city of Vilnius is the historic capital of the Grand Duchy of Lithuania, an entity that also encompassed Belarus, and was for centuries closely associated with Poland. The Lithuanian and Belarusian nobility of the area were polonized centuries ago, and Poles became the leading ethnic group in the city. After World War I, Vilnius was seized by the Poles and remained in their possession until Poland's defeat in 1939, when it was handed to Lithuania by Stalin, and then swallowed up by the USSR along with the rest of Lithuania in 1940. During the war, the city's large Jewish population was annihilated by the Germans, and after the war the bulk of the better-educated Polish population left for Poland. The remaining Poles found themselves under double rule: by the titular nationality, the Lithuanians, and by the Russians, representing the Union. It was only in the late 1980s, after the Lithuanian independence movement began to gain strength, that Moscow decided to play the Polish card. The Polish community became divided: some favored Lithuania's independence, others clamored for a national-territorial unit of their own. For its part, Poland was clearly against the establishment of a "Polish Republic" within Lithuania, an idea with some unedifying precedents from the 1920s. Still, Lithuania's many mistakes in the treatment of Poles in the Vilnius region, ranging from the eradication of symbols of the Vilnius Polish past to job discrimination, did little to relieve the situation.

The case of the Tajiks in Uzbekistan and the Uzbeks in Kyrgyzstan follows another pattern. The borders between the Central Asian republics as drawn in 1924–25 respected ethnic lines in rural areas but neglected historic ties and ignored the urban ethnic balance. In the decades since then, the total population has practically tripled and many demographic shifts have taken place. By now, many borders in Central Asia can easily be contested, and minorities within all the republics can present legitimate claims against the titular nationalities. The situation is even more complicated by the fact that the Kremlin used the region as a dumping ground for the whole USSR. It is an area into which several deported nationalities were dropped alongside the victims of all kinds of purges, including Tatars from the Crimea, Meskhetian Turks from the Georgian-Turkish border region, Volga Germans, and Ukrainian "kulaks." Today, with Central Asia increasingly afflicted by overpopulation, ecological problems, economic difficulties, and social and political conflicts, ethnic tensions are on the rise.

Paradoxically, the failure of the August 1991 coup and the ensuing collapse of the USSR only complicates the situation of minority nationalities within the former Soviet Union. The responsibility for interethnic peace has moved from the center and into the lap of individual republics. How the minorities within the republics will fare under the new conditions is another matter.

5

Russians in Central Asia and Kazakhstan

Kazakhstan and four Central Asian republics have large Russian populations whose situations vary from republic to republic. Northern Kazakhstan, which borders Siberia, was subjected to gradual Russian penetration in the eighteenth and nineteenth centuries. Waves of Russian and Ukrainian settlers pushed Kazakhs out of many areas, to the point that until recently Russians outnumbered the Kazakh population. Large Russian settlements were also established in the southeastern corner of Kazakhstan, along the Syr-Darya River, and in northern Kyrgyzstan. The Slavs dominated not only mining and industry, two fields established by Russian capital, but also agriculture; only cattle-breeding remained fully in the hands of the traditionally nomadic Kazakhs and Kyrgyzes. Local cities most often developed out of Russian outposts, since the Kazakhs and the Kyrgyzes did not have an urban culture.

In terms of ethnic distribution, Kazakhstan can be divided into three belts: the predominantly Russian north, the sparsely populated "hungry steppe" in the middle, and the Kazakh-Kyrgyz south, a great part of which was under the control of the neighboring khans of Kokand until 1865. In the southwestern corner, the so-called Semireche Cossacks were settled by the tsarist government in the last quarter of the nineteenth century (with the influx ending during World War I).

By contrast, Turkestan, or Central Asia proper (that is, the territory conquered between 1865 and 1885), attracted almost exclusively urban Russian settlers. The settlers built new towns at the edges of the old ones, creating an architectural separateness resembling the pattern in North Africa under French domination. Still, the number of Russians was relatively small: insignificant in the semi-autonomous protectorates of Khiva and Bukhara, and only 6.4 percent of the total population in the general-governorship of Turkestan (including Semireche) in 1911.

During the revolution, the Russian city-dwellers and railroad workers in Tashkent became the backbone of the Turkestan Soviet regime, which from the outset maintained a strong colonialist orientation. The Bolsheviks' espousal of "dictatorship of the proletariat" in a region where the proletariat was for all intents and purposes non-native became a justification for maintaining Russian control over the political structure, at least until the collapse of the *basmachi* revolt. There was a short interlude in the 1920s during which local Muslim cadres prospered. It was followed by the collectivization drive of the late 1920s and the subsequent purges of nationalist leaders in the 1930s, which coincided with the arrival of new waves of Russian and Ukrainian settlers: "kulak" families deported by the regime and sent for resettlement to Central Asia; industrial workers recruited for the massive construction projects of the five-year plans; and families of the victims of a succession of Stalinist purges. During World War II new waves of population were channeled into the area, ranging from entire "punished peoples" deported by Stalin, to Polish, Baltic, and Jewish war refugees.

This massive injection of outsiders created a very unusual situation, blending the atmosphere of pre-independence Algeria, with *pieds noirs* dominating over the Muslims, and that of Siberia, with its generations of pioneers and deportees.

The contemporary Russian population of Central Asia falls into four categories:

Table 12

Russians in Central Asia and Kazakhstan
(in percent of population of the republic)

Republic	1926	1939	1959	1970	1979	1989
Uzbekistan	5.4	11.5	13.5	12.5	10.8	8.3
Turkmenistan	8.2	21.6	17.3	14.5	12.6	9.5
Tajikistan	0.7	9.1	13.3	11.9	10.4	7.6
Kyrgyzstan	11.7	20.8	30.2	27.0	25.9	21.4
Kazakhstan	19.7	40.3	42.7	42.4	40.8	37.7
Ukrainians in Kazakhstan	n.d.	13.3	10.8	8.8	7.2	6.1

1. "Colonial" cadres who served the Soviet command-and-control apparatus. Backed up by Moscow, their job was simultaneously to assist local Muslim cadres and to watch over them.
2. Engineers and technicians, who ran the bulk of industry and the transportation and communications systems.
3. Industrial workers, who still account for the majority of the skilled labor force and as such are indispensable to the economy of the region.
4. Russians employed in menial blue- and white-collar jobs, who could relatively easily be replaced by native Central Asians.

Of the four categories, it is obvious that the Russian "colonial" elite, the party officials delegated to keep the area under Moscow's control, is on the way out, or at least out of power. Political clout is now squarely in Muslim hands, and Russian officials have no choice but to pack their suitcases. Deprived of their protection, the mass of Russian settlers will finally have to face reality. The technical group, although vulnerable, has value to the newly independent regimes and has not been so directly menaced. The third and especially the fourth group are power-

Table 13

Russians in Kazakhstan, by Region (1989)

Region	Population (000)	% Russians	% Kazakhs
Aktiubinsk	733	23.7	55.6
Eastern Kazakhstan	931	65.9	37.2
Karaganda	1,348	52.2	17.2
Kokchetai	662	39.5	28.9
Kustanai	1,223	43.7	22.9
Pavlodar	942	45.4	28.5
Northern Kazakhstan	600	62.1	18.6
Semipalatinsk	834	36.0	51.9
Ural	629	34.4	55.8
Tselinograd	1,003	44.7	22.4

Source: 1989 census.

less. In a region where unemployment is already sky-high, un-skilled or unneeded Russians have little choice but to leave or face misery. They are clear candidates for outmigration, and many of them have already taken that path.

By and large, local Russians have not organized "interfronts" on the model of their Baltic counterparts. The exceptions are in the city of Tashkent and in Kazakhstan, where Russians and other Slavs are concentrated and have engaged in some common action. But it is clear to most that strong-hand action would be counterproductive: the demographic realities are too unfavorable to the Russians.

The Russian population in northern Kazakhstan and in parts of Kyrgyzstan has somewhat better prospects. Not only do Russians constitute the majority in these areas, but Kazakh authorities, fearful of possible Russian demands for the transfer of northern territories, are inclined to go easy with "nativization." Russian communities will be able to elect their own local officials. But outside of these areas there is little future for Russian settlers in Central Asia and Kazakhstan, notwithstanding their membership in the Moscow-dominated Commonwealth of Independent States. If the examples of North Africa and the Middle East teach us anything, it is that the bulk of European settlers, businessmen and technicians excepted, have no place in independent Muslim states, the latter being ill-disposed to any kind of American-style multicultural experience.

6

Russians in the Baltic States

Russian settlement in the Baltic region started with the Russian conquest, which took place in stages throughout the eighteenth century. Nevertheless, by the time of the October 1917 revolution, the Russian population was quite small, except in the city of Riga.

After the revolution, a certain number of Russian refugees arrived, but most were en route to the West, and few stayed. By 1940, when the Baltic states were annexed by the USSR, the number of Russians was still small. Moreover, some "old Russians" either fled westward or were deported along with their Baltic neighbors by the Soviet authorities.

After the Soviet reoccupation of the Baltic lands in 1944, a policy of steady settlement of Russians was implemented. First, officials and military personnel arrived with their families; then came workers hired by the newly established heavy and defense industries; and finally, settlers moved into areas depopulated by the war, such as the northeastern corner of Estonia and the city of Vilnius—the first devastated by war, the second by the Nazi genocide of the Jewish population and the postwar outmigration of many Poles. One of the key attractions of the Baltic republics was their relatively high standard of living, which was a product of their independent past and survival of the work ethic (and not, as many Russians assumed, of Soviet generosity).

Table 14

Russians in the Baltic Republics (in percent of population)

	1930s	1959	1989
Lithuania	2.4[a]	8.8	9.3
Latvia	10.6[b]	26.4	33.8
Estonia	8.5[c]	20.1	30.3

[a] In 1939, without the Wilno (Vilnius) region.
[b] In 1935, with the small territory ceded to RSFSR in the 1940s.
[c] In 1934, with the two districts ceded to RSFSR in the 1940s.

The low birthrates among Latvians and Estonians were another factor that helped to increase the proportion of Russians in these republics. Only Catholic Lithuania was able to hold its own after the initial Russian influx. A significant concentration of all-Union industrial enterprises, directly subordinated to Moscow, attracted additional Russian personnel. By 1990 Russians predominated in the population of northeastern Estonia and shared the city of Tallinn with native Estonians. In Vilnius they made up a quarter of the population. Russians predominated in Riga and accounted for a third of the total population of Latvia (more if Ukrainians and Belarusians are added).

The Russian-speaking population in the Baltic republics may be divided into several groups:

1. Old-timers whose families settled in the area prior to World War II, who know the local languages, understand local customs, and generally sympathize with the Baltic peoples.
2. Those postwar immigrants who were attracted by the freer atmosphere and Western way of life in the Baltic and who now also tend to sympathize with the native majority.
3. Moscow-dispatched *apparatchiki* and their families, whose allegiance has always been to the center and who have never bothered to learn the local languages or customs. They clearly side against local aspirations.
4. The mass of Russian *"Gastarbeiter,"* industrial workers at-

tracted by higher living standards, who barely recognized that they were working in another republic. They now feel economically threatened and react accordingly.

During the Gorbachev years, Russian military officers and other functionaries (active and retired) were in the forefront organizing Russian workers for the struggle against Baltic independence. They played on a whole array of anxieties: fear of expulsion, distrust of privatization, worry about job security, and so forth.

Moscow supported the anti-independence groups through a variety of means, ranging from financial assistance to propaganda campaigns, and finally through sporadic military intervention in their favor. Russian workers employed by the enterprises of all-Union importance were mobilized by their bosses to attend "spontaneous" anti-independence demonstrations. Strikes were orchestrated and defiance of elected authorities was encouraged. The Russian "interfronts" became Moscow's strong arm in the Baltic republics, wielded to stop secession at any price. In addition, Soviet troops were used to "protect" the buildings "belonging" to pro-Moscow factions within the Communist Party— groups made up almost exclusively of Russians, plus a few native collaborators showcased for propaganda purposes.

The Baltic national fronts, for their part, made their own mistakes in handling the Russian minority. Discussions of limiting future citizenship to those who had held it prior to 1940 (and their families) deflected a good number of potential Russian sympathizers. Measures directed at a speedy shift of all government work and official communications from Russian to the local language also frightened the postwar Russian migrants. Estonian, an especially difficult language for an outsider to learn, was seen as a barrier that few Russian-speaking settlers would be willing or able to overcome.

The future of Russian settlers in the Baltic states is still uncertain. Russians, already compromised by their anti-independence activities, could fall victim to local revenge. On the other hand, the support given by Boris Yeltsin, as president of the Russian Federation, to the Baltic struggle for independence was a positive precedent. The strategy of transforming the Baltic states into commercial beachheads for Western trade with Russia might also dissipate the spirit of revenge. The massive transit of Russian nonferrous metals to the West via Tallinn in 1992 is a good example.

Still, Russian immigration into the area must come to an end. Repatriation incentives are being offered and citizenship for post-1940 Russian immigrants is being restricted. Persons in this category, as well as their descendants, are not automatically granted citizenship, but must apply for it within a specific time. Former KGB and party officials, people with criminal records, individuals who actively opposed a republic's drive for independence, and in some cases even chronic alcoholics are excluded. In addition, there are minimum residence requirements for potential candidates for citizenship, ranging from sixteen years of residence in Latvia to only two in Estonia. All post-1940 arrivals were excluded from taking part in referendums that deal with citizenship issues.

The final factor at play in the Baltic is the continuing presence in Latvia and Estonia of Russian troops, which President Boris Yeltsin has refused to withdraw until the rights of the Russian population have been satisfactorily guaranteed. Russian troops were pulled out of Lithuania. Given the electoral defeat of Lithuania's Sajudis national front government, as well as the Russian military presence in Kaliningrad, along Lithuania's western border, this was a concession that Moscow could well afford to make.

7

Russians in Ukraine and Belarus

The problem of Russians in Ukraine and Belarus is a crucial issue in Russian-Ukrainian and Russian-Belarusian relations. Russians are substantial minorities in these republics, accounting for roughly one out of every five inhabitants. Russians constitute the majority of the urban population of eastern (left-bank) and southern Ukraine and almost half the population of the industrial Don basin. In addition, they outnumber Ukrainians three to one in the Crimea. In the West, in the former Galicia and in Transcarpathian Ukraine, the number of Russians is insignificant. The pattern of Russian concentration in Ukraine is due to the fact that between the second part of the thirteenth century and the seventeenth century, the eastern areas of today's Ukraine were a very sparsely populated no-man's-land between Muscovy, Poland, and the Crimean khanate. When Tatar power was on the decline, settlers from both Russia and Ukraine (the latter was still in Polish-Lithuanian hands) began to move into the area, and with the conquest of Crimea at the end of the eighteenth century, the same movement took place there too. Thus cut off from Kievan Ukraine, local Ukrainians underwent a centuries-long russification.

In the latter part of the seventeenth century, Moscow began to push the Poles westward, and Russian settlers followed the

Table 15

Russians in Areas of Their Largest Concentration in Ukraine (1989)

Region	Russian population (in 000)	% Russians	% Ukrainians
Donetsk	2,316	43.6	50.7
Zaporozhe	664	32.0	63.1
Lugansk	1,289	44.8	51.9
Crimea	1,630	67.0	25.8
City of Kiev	534	21.0	72.0

Sources: 1989 census and Mikhail Guboglo, "Demography and Language in the Capitals of the Union Republics," *Journal of Soviet Nationalities,* vol. 1, no. 4, p. 11.

troops. On the other hand, the areas that remained in Polish hands until the eighteenth-century partitions of Poland absorbed far fewer Russian settlers, even after their annexation by Russia. Areas that fell into Austro-Hungarian hands (namely Galicia) obviously saw no Russian settlers until World War II.

Russians in the Crimea or in eastern Ukraine never felt that they lived in an alien land, and regarded the Ukrainians as colorful and sympathetic peasants speaking a local dialect of Russian. Russians in central Ukraine had a more pronounced feeling of difference, but, being concentrated exclusively in the cities, they tended to see this as an urban-rural distinction rather than a national one. In the west, however, the picture was totally different. There, Russians were mostly *chinovniki* (functionaries) and their families, and were placed amidst the mass of Ukrainian peasantry, Jewish shtetl-dwellers, and Polish noblemen, with each group maintaining its own separateness. They saw Ukrainians as being similar to Russians in culture, language, and religion, but still very different.

The gap between the Russians and the Ukrainians is most obvious when we look at attitudes toward liberty, authority, and individual freedom. The Russian tradition tends to equate liberty with chaos, freedom with license, and authority with law and order. Ukrainian traditions are different. Nourished by Cossack

Table 16

Russians in Ukraine and Belarus (all groups in percent)

	1959			1979			1989		
	N	R	O	N	R	O	N	R	O
Ukraine	76.8	16.9	6.3	73.6	21.0	5.3	72.2	21.9	5.9
Belarus	81.1	8.2	10.7	79.4	11.9	8.7	77.4	17.1	5.5

Key:
N: Natives (Ukrainians or Belarusians, in their respective republics).
R: Russians.
O: Others, including Ukrainians in Belarus or Belarusians in Ukraine.

freedoms, the liberties enjoyed by the petty nobility in the Polish-Lithuanian state of which Ukraine was for so long a part, and a distrust of absolute authority, the Ukrainians remained attached to their freedom-loving past. Their linguistic and cultural closeness to Moscow could never fully bridge that gap.

Solzhenitsyn's vision of a post-Soviet Slavic state made up of three eastern Slavic nations stirred resentment among many Ukrainians, although it was warmly endorsed by Russian settlers. Russians see Ukraine as so closely interconnected with Russia that any attempt to sever the links could be fatal to both, while for most Ukrainians, the embrace seems too tight. They prefer a relationship based on friendship, equality, and sovereignty, more along the lines of the 1990 Russian-Ukrainian bilateral treaty. But even with full Ukrainian independence, it is unlikely that Russian inhabitants will leave the republic the way they are leaving Central Asia and Transcaucasia. The future of Russians in Ukraine lies in continued association with their Ukrainian neighbors and final abandonment of old assumptions of Russian cultural and political superiority.

In Belarus, Russians are more evenly distributed across the country, although similarly concentrated in the cities. Their position is stronger than in Ukraine, despite the fact that they account for only one out of every nine inhabitants (roughly half their proportion in Ukraine). This is mostly due to the fact that Belarusian national consciousness is weaker than Ukrainian: many Belarusians share Russian prejudices about the Belarusian language and culture, which they see in folkloric terms. One out of seven Belarusians lists Russian as his mother tongue, and almost everyone speaks Russian fluently. The fact that all of Belarus was once part of the Grand Duchy of Lithuania, and later part of the Polish-Lithuanian state, seems to have left a mark only on the western border areas, which between the two world wars were part of the reborn Polish state. In the rest of Belarus, Russians feel as at home as in eastern Ukraine. It is only after the Chernobyl catastrophe, which impacted large areas of southeastern Belarus and weakened local confidence in Moscow, that national feelings were aroused, propelling Belarus on the road to sovereignty.

8

Inter-Republican Migration

Past inter-republican migration processes in the USSR fell into three main categories: deportation, organized migration, and spontaneous migration. During Stalin's time, deportation accounted for a good part of the migration total. Organized migration continued under Khrushchev and Brezhnev. But today, as at the outset of the Soviet regime, migration is almost entirely spontaneous, the state having finally withdrawn from the process.

Stalin-era deportations displaced millions of people, sometimes entire nations. The first massive shift of population was the shipping of the upper layers of the peasantry (the so-called kulaks) to labor camps and the resettlement of their families in Siberia, Kazakhstan, and Central Asia. This altered the ethnic balance in Kazakhstan and tremendously increased the number of Russians and Ukrainians in the rest of Central Asia. Continuous purges from 1926 to 1939 injected five million people into the same regions. After the implementation of the Soviet-German Non-Aggression Pact, Poles, Lithuanians, Latvians, Estonians, and Moldavians followed. Then, during the war, "punished peoples" were shipped in the same direction. At the time of his death in 1953, Stalin was busy preparing another shipment, this time of Jews to the Far East (probably to Birobijan), a feat he lacked time to implement.

State-sponsored organized migration was based not on compulsion, but on inducement, sometimes accompanied by pressure. Among the larger ones, one might mention the big "stroikas" (large-scale construction projects), which targeted Komsomol members, or the Virgin Lands settlement program of Nikita Khrushchev. Massive hirings at all-Union enterprises in the Baltic republics, the attempt to repopulate the non–black-soil regions of central Russia, inducements offered to lure demobilized draftees from the Central Asian republics to labor-short industrial areas, and measures to attract more laborers to Siberia are among the best-known organized migration schemes. The German-funded resettlement of Soviet military families now leaving eastern Germany as well as the other former Warsaw Pact states is another example of organized migration, albeit different in kind.

Spontaneous migration processes involving the movement of individuals (with or without families) from labor-rich to labor-short areas (for example, the non–black-soil zone of Russia) are beneficial as far as manpower problems are concerned. In this respect, migration between areas presenting similar labor situations, such as from Uzbekistan to Tajikistan or from Moscow to Petersburg, and vice versa, is neutral. Negative migration processes involve movement in the "wrong" direction (from the standpoint of manpower requirements), for example, emigration from Siberia, or the abandonment of villages in the non–black-soil areas of Russia, or moving to crowded Moscow.

Of course, the big cities, the Baltic republics, and Crimea have always been attractive to voluntary migrants. The capital cities (especially Moscow, but also Leningrad, Kiev, Tashkent, and Baku) offered a lively cosmopolitan atmosphere and the advantage of better supplies. Although the right to reside in those cities was officially restricted (job, lodging, and residence permit to be procured simultaneously), the numbers of registered and unregistered inhabitants grew constantly, with large numbers of "illegals" finding havens in the surrounding small towns and villages.

The Baltic republics were attractive for their higher quality of

Table 17

Russians in the Capitals of the Former Union Republics (1989)

City (capital of)	Titular nationality	Russians		Others
		% of the total	% speaking the language of the titular nationality	
Moscow (Russia)	89.6	89.6	—	10.4[a]
Kiev (Ukraine)	72.4	20.9	47.3	6.7[b]
Minsk (Belarus)	72.1	20.0	24.8	7.9[c]
Kishinev (Moldova)	49.2	26.4	11.1	24.4[d]
Vilnius (Lithuania)	50.5	20.2	31.6	29.3[e]
Riga (Latvia)	36.5	47.3	19.6	16.2[f]
Tallinn (Estonia)	47.4	41.2	15.4	11.4[g]
Erevan (Armenia)	96.5	1.9	43.3	1.6
Baku (Azerbaijan)	61.8	18.0	12.2	20.2[h]
Tbilisi (Georgia)	66.0	10.0	34.5	24.0[i]
Tashkent (Uzbekistan)	44.2	34.0	3.5	21.8[j]
Alma-Ata (Kazakhstan)	22.5	59.1	0.6	18.4[k]
Bishkek (Kyrgyzstan)	22.7	55.8	0.6	21.5[l]
Dushanbe (Tajikistan)	38.3	32.8	2.3	28.9[m]
Ashkhabad (Turkmenistan)	50.8	32.4	1.7	16.8[n]

Sources: 1989 census, and Mikhail Guboglo, "Demography and Language in the Capitals of the Union Republics," *Journal of Soviet Nationalities*, vol. 1, no. 4 (1990).

Notes: "Others" include:

[a] 2.9 percent Ukrainians and 2 percent Jews;
[b] 3.9 percent Jews;
[c] 3.2 percent Ukrainians and 2.5 percent Jews;
[d] 14.3 percent Ukrainians and 5.4 percent Jews;
[e] 18.8 percent Poles and 5.3 percent Belarusians;
[f] 4.8 percent Ukrainians and 4.8 percent Belarusians;
[g] 4.8 percent Ukrainians and 2.6 percent Belarusians;
[h] 12.2 percent Armenians (very few remained in 1992);
[i] 12.1 percent Armenians;
[j] 6.3 percent Tatars and 2.9 percent Ukrainians;
[k] 4.1 percent Ukrainians and 3.7 percent Uigurs;
[l] 5.6 percent Ukrainians and 5.8 percent Tatars;
[m] 10.6 percent Uzbeks and 4.1 percent Tatars;
[n] 4.6 percent Armenians and 2.7 percent Ukrainians.

life and more European standards in terms of culture, organization, sanitation, and so on. Military retirees in search of greater comfort, intellectuals seeking a more Western atmosphere, and industrial workers and peasants fleeing the poverty of neighboring Russian and Belarusian villages were all drawn to the Baltic region.

Areas in need of massive immigration, such as Siberia and central Russia, experienced great difficulties attracting permanent settlers. Substandard housing, grim surroundings, and the harsh climate of much of Siberia created insurmountable obstacles, poorly remediated by insufficiently enhanced salaries. Attempts to draw surplus labor from rural Central Asia failed. Unwillingness to leave native villages and the Muslim milieu, compounded by the unattractiveness of Russian industrial and mining complexes, worked against a repetition of the south-to-north migration pattern so familiar in the Western world. On the contrary, prior to the 1980s, labor-rich Central Asia was still attracting immigrants.

One can only speculate about the possible consequences of any future lifting of the registration requirement (*propiska*) that has inhibited migration to the large cities. Such a change may affect internal migration patterns within a republic, but it is unlikely to alter the present trend toward ethnic consolidation, especially as new obstacles to inter-republican migration are erected.

Obratnichestvo (remigration to old homelands) is the prevailing trend of the current decade. Thousands of families are leaving their present residence in order to return to the land of their grandfathers, which often they have never seen. The myth about the "Soviet people, a new community of nations living in one Soviet fatherland," has fallen by the wayside. Since the explosion of ethnic tensions in the late 1980s, and especially since the beginning of the new decade, inter-republican migration has been governed more by fear of ethnic violence than by economic considerations. Armenians are fleeing from Azerbaijan, Azeris from Armenia, Meskhetians from Uzbekistan, Russians and Ukrainians from rural Uzbekistan and Tajikistan, and so forth, while

Table 18

Net Slavic Outmigration from Two Central Asian Republics
(in thousands)

	Uzbekistan	Kyrgyzstan
1992	73.6	55.9
1991	25.0	11.6
1990	42.0	17.2
1989	18.6	2.4

Source: Central Statistical Agency of Uzbekistan and Kyrgyzstan State Statistical Agency, as quoted by Peter Sinnott, Columbia University, at a conference on the Emergence of a New State System in Central Asia, December 3–4, 1993.

migration into the Baltic republics has practically ceased. Unless ethnic strife subsides and the economic conditions that are exacerbating interethnic tensions dramatically improve, the current migration trends will probably continue for the rest of the decade.

The result is that the former Soviet Union has a refugee problem unlike anything experienced since the flight from the German advance during World War II. Soviet authorities were utterly unprepared to handle the emergency when it began in 1988. In Moscow, where many refugees ended up, the situation quickly became unmanageable given the shortage of housing, the frequent hostility of a local population already fed up with queues and goods "deficits," the lack of civic associations capable of rendering assistance, and the bureaucratic maze. In Azerbaijan and in Armenia, which was only beginning to cope with the effects of a devastating earthquake, refugees soon overtaxed the local facilities and set themselves up in shantytowns in and around urban areas. The refugee problem in both republics added to the economic disarray, which in turn created new waves of refugees in both directions. It also produced political consequences, ultimately bringing nationalist forces to power in both republics.

The small number of Armenians who reached Central Asia after a trans-Caspian exodus from Baku were the cause of tension

---

Table 19

Influx of Refugees to Russia

Total in July 1992: 11,813
Total in August 1992: 23,423

Among them:	
from Azerbaijan	6,071
from Georgia	5,191
from Moldova	2,463
from Chechnia	1,587
from Tajikistan	5,747

Source: *Argumenty i fakty*, 1992, no. 40 (October).

---

in Dushanbe (the capital of Tajikistan) when a rumor spread that they would be granted housing with priority over Tajiks. The ensuing riot resulted in bloodshed, the departure of Armenians, and a partial flight of Russian settlers frightened by the events. Communist authorities in Dushanbe had a difficult time recovering from the shock and lost power in the fall of 1992 as the country descended into a period of violent internal conflict.

In Georgia, the ongoing ethnic violence in Abkhazia and southern Ossetia created thousands of refugees. Anticommunist nationalists gained power in the 1990 elections in Georgia, but their intolerance of ideological "enemies" (as well as minority "aliens") brought disfavor. In 1992, moderate elements drove nationalist leader Zviad Gamsakhurdia from power and installed former Soviet Foreign Minister Eduard Shevardnadze in the presidency, but failed to reverse the military losses.

In Central Asia, violence between the Uzbeks, the largest national group in the area, and their neighbors (Kyrgyzes in the Fergana valley, Meskhetian Turks deported to that same area, Tajiks in the towns of the former Emirate of Bukhara) added new refugees to the total numbers. The Meskhetians departed for Azerbaijan. (Georgia, where they dwelled prior to World War II, refused to accept them.) Many Russian rural settlers, especially from the Kara-Kalpak ASSR, moved either to Russia or to Tashkent. Crimean Tatars sought return to their Crimean homeland, where they faced hostility in their old hometowns and settled in shantytowns around them.

In the Baltic republics, thanks to the remarkable discipline shown by the local population, conscious of the need not to provoke Moscow, the Russian minority was never in physical danger and only rarely sought refuge elsewhere. On the contrary, many Russians tried to gain permits to settle in Estonia or Latvia, hoping to leave the USSR with the departing republics.

The refugee problem has magnified ethnic intolerance. Each republic is becoming more monoethnic and whatever integration was achieved during the decades past is being reversed.

The events of August 1991 and their aftermath accelerated the trends already under way. Outmigration of non-natives from ethnic conflict zones is gaining momentum. *Obratnichestvo* from Central Asia will grow in proportion to the weakening of inter-republican ties, and would probably continue even if the situation were to stabilize.

A great deal of population movement is expected from Ukraine, Belarus, and Lithuania into Poland, although mostly for a temporary stay. Already millions of "Soviets" visit Poland every year: most of them come to trade, some to work for convertible Polish zlotys, and a few as refugees trying to transit to the West. With Polish salaries much greater than ruble salaries in dollar terms, the temptation is great. A similar trend exists between Estonia and Finland, albeit on a much smaller scale. The vision of Soviet refugees, "guest workers," and "tourists" arriving by the millions haunts the chancelleries of Western Europe, and Poland is now being pressured to reduce transit opportunities for Soviet visitors.

Part 3

Issues

1

The Legacy of Soviet Federalism

The fate of Soviet federalism is a unique example of the triumph of form over content. The system assigned almost every nationality in the Soviet Union to one of four categories of national autonomy and gave each autonomous unit an array of apparently substantial, but very vaguely defined, rights. The component nationalities of the USSR were granted all the paraphernalia of government and numerous symbols of statehood, but had only the most limited ability to exercise the corresponding rights without Kremlin approval. The elements tying the whole system together were (1) the Communist Party, with its centralized apparatus and discipline; (2) the Party's swords, the Soviet army and the security forces; and (3) the planned economic system, which constricted the freedom of action of all republics, exercised strict control over the budget, and ruled directly over large industrial complexes located on republican territory (the so-called enterprises of all-Union importance).

On an individual level, the members of "titular" nationalities enjoyed privileged access to jobs and educational opportunities within their national-territorial units, as well as relative equality elsewhere. There were two types of exceptions—"punished peoples" and Jews, who saw their rights limited on national grounds; and strategically implanted Russian officials, who enjoyed special privileges in the national republics—but these involved relatively small numbers of people.

Fifteen union republics, twenty autonomous republics, eight autonomous regions, and ten national districts made up the four levels of national autonomy. With each step down, the rights enjoyed by the autonomous entity were reduced, while with each step up they increased. Within each level, every nation enjoyed the same rights (or lack of them), regardless of the size of its population, territory, or level of advancement. For many of the component nations, Soviet-type autonomy was the first experience of statehood. For others, it was the privation of national independence. Some nations were given more status than they aspired to; others saw their status reduced below their initial expectations. The Baltic republics suffered the loss of their hard-won independence; the Tajiks enjoyed a form of statehood for the first time; and the Chukchi found themselves endowed with more state's rights than they had ever imagined. The Lithuanians were territorially satisfied; the Tajiks remained with pending claims against the Uzbeks (with whom they previously shared their statehood); while the Georgians had to accept the creation of three smaller autonomies within their own borders.

Every republic had its own Communist Party structures, modeled along the lines of the center's, albeit at lower levels. Each had a party first secretary and a party central committee with a presidium (analogous to the Politburo in Moscow). Elections were shams: the party nomenklatura ruled the land. Central control was always present. Russian *apparatchiki* watched over the native cadres, who were allowed to fill their pockets in return for letting Moscow pull the strings.

The republic governments were likewise limited replicas of the central government. Within the governmental set-up there were three types of ministries: ministries in charge of local matters; mixed ministries, which operated at both the federal and local levels, with the latter subordinated to the former; and Union ministries, which existed only at the center but exercised direct control over local enterprises under their jurisdiction. (Heavy industry, for example, was centrally run.) Republic-level ministers enjoyed their titles, their furnished offices, their staffs, their perquisites, and other accoutrements of high function. Thus the forms of statehood were there, though they had little substance.

Each union republic was provided with its own university (if none had been previously established), and each enjoyed the right to establish an Academy of Sciences of its own (whether or not the level of art and science in the republic justified this). In the institutions of higher learning there were parallel Russian and national sections, each working in its own language, with the Russian section in less advanced republics being academically far ahead.

But the national nomenklatura had a counteradvantage that Moscow never really overcame: it was able to create local loyalties, amass material resources, and buy the silence of Moscow's agents with bribes and pay-offs. The native masses, regardless of their attitude toward the system, preferred local bosses over Russian outsiders. The facade of local control over the party and the government apparatus, which so long obscured the reality of central authority, little by little acquired a life of its own. Thus an entire local apparatus of governance found itself properly placed, properly titled, and furnished with the symbols of statehood, ready to assume power if the appropriate circumstances were ever to occur.

This opportunity presented itself during the years of Gorbachev's perestroika, which failed in its attempt to reform the system, but removed its teeth and weakened its ability to control the component republics. During the Brezhnev years and the interregnum between Brezhnev and Gorbachev, almost no one, either in the East or in the West (except for Hélène Carrère d'Encausse and a very few others), was aware of the potentially disintegrationist features of the Soviet federal system, the built-in weakness that stemmed from the contradiction between the form and the substance. But form won over substance, and the Soviet federal structure came apart as soon as it came alive.

2

Border Disputes

Many of the border disputes that now plague the post-Soviet states are a reflection of changes in the ethnodemographic picture since the time the inter-republican borders were drawn. For a long time, of course, those boundaries were purely administrative dividers rather than borders between sovereign entities. In some areas of the country, especially in Central Asia and Siberia, borders between the newly created national-territorial units were drawn without historic precedents.

Stalin's successors sometimes seemed to want to wish away the basic elements of Soviet federal structure. Khrushchev, for example, toyed with the idea of abolishing the republics altogether. Brezhnev claimed to foresee the speedy merger of all the component nations of the USSR into "one Soviet people, a new community of nations." Certainly, Gorbachev little expected that his liberalization would awaken national feelings and a fuller consciousness of national-territorial integrity. The truth began to dawn in the late 1980s as a number of border conflicts heated up.

Nagorno-Karabakh: Azeris and Armenians have now been engaged in armed conflict over Nagorno-Karabakh for several years (the background of the crisis was discussed in part 1, chapter 5). Economics and geography favor Azerbaijan, demography favors Armenia, while historical justifications abound on both

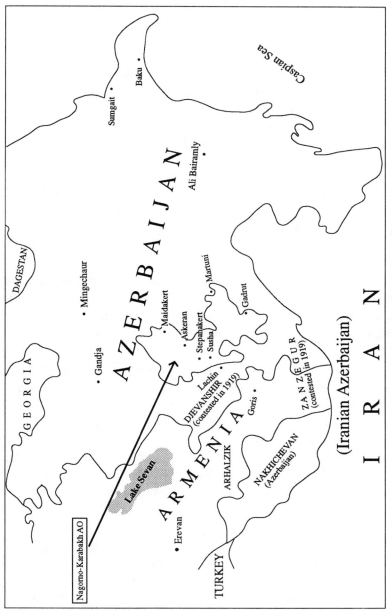

Armenian-Azeri Conflict

sides, depending on the century in question. The dispute managed for a time to reverse the historical attitudes of both nations toward Russia: traditionally pro-Russian Armenia began to lean toward independence, while the Azeri leadership sided with Kremlin conservatives (mostly, although not exclusively, to be on the opposite side from the Armenians). After the failed putsch the situation reversed itself, with Armenia seeking Russian protection and Azerbaijan looking to Turkey.

The location of the Nagorno-Karabakh Autonomous Region makes it difficult if not impossible to transfer the area from Azeri to Armenian jurisdiction without violating geographic reality as well as the economic unity of the old Khanate of Karabakh. This is a common problem with borders drawn in the USSR in the 1920s: they were meant to follow the principle of "national delimitation," disregarding such natural dividers as mountain chains and rivers and ignoring the problem of access. Many boundaries were drawn the way gerrymandered electoral districts are concocted in the United States. When borders were a sheer formality this was not a serious problem; but when they became real, their entangled nature complicated interstate relations.

The Caucasus: The northern borders of Georgia follow the mountain chain of the Caucasus and are historically and economically justified. Any revision would violate these basic principles. However, in its desire to arrest the Georgian drive to independence, the Kremlin encouraged separatism in the two autonomous units within Georgia located south of the mountains, namely Abkhazia and Ossetia. The cases are quite different. In Abkhazia, the titular nationality constitutes a minority (only 20 percent), the Georgians are in the majority, and there is a significant Russian population. In the South Ossetian Autonomous Region, the Ossetians are in the majority. However, Abkhazia is geographically on the northwestern edge of Georgia and not essential to the country's integrity, while South Ossetia drives a wedge into the heart of Georgia. Its unification with North Ossetia (an autonomous republic within the Russian Federation) would be unacceptable to Georgia. Thus the Georgians oppose Abkhazian secession on demographic grounds and South Ossetian secession on geopolitical grounds. Georgian internal squabbles make things even worse.

The border imbroglio in the North Caucasus is the result of numerous border shifts in the 1920s, 1930s, and late 1950s. The temporary erasure of several national-territorial units from the map in the wake of Stalin's World War II deportations of Chechens, Ingushes, Balkars, and Karachais (see part 2, chapter 1, on "punished peoples") created additional problems: the restored units were reborn in altered borders.

North Ossetia, which enjoyed Stalin's favor, at first gained at the expense of all her "punished" neighbors and even received a Cossack area from Stavropol Krai (Territory). Upon their return to the region under Khrushchev's amnesty, the Chechens were given in compensation another slice of Cossack lands, plus a piece of Dagestan. The latter, in turn, received a large chunk of Stavropol Krai, including the Russian-populated city of Kizliar. Such "gifts" of Russian land were very much in line with Khrushchev's belief in the imminent disappearance of national-territorial borders and the desirability of spreading Russians among non-Russians in order to consolidate the Union.

At present, not only are several areas in the North Caucasus being contested, but some artificial binational units have either split or are in the process of splitting (including the Chechen-Ingush and Karachai-Balkar combinations). Coexistence becomes too especially difficult in a chauvinistic climate.

The Status of Vilnius (Wilno, Vilna): This ancient capital of the Grand Duchy of Lithuania is dear to three nations: Lithuania, Poland, and Belarus. Founded by Lithuanian rulers, and subjected first to Belarusian, then to Polish cultural impact, Wilno's influence covered the enormous area between Bialystok and Smolensk (from northeastern Poland to Russian lands beyond the borders of Belarus). The city also became the "Jerusalem" of Lithuania, the cultural and religious center of the region's Jewry.

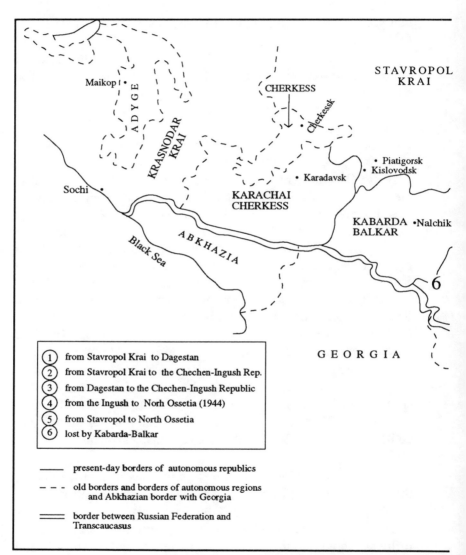

① from Stavropol Krai to Dagestan
② from Stavropol Krai to the Chechen-Ingush Rep.
③ from Dagestan to the Chechen-Ingush Republic
④ from the Ingush to Norh Ossetia (1944)
⑤ from Stavropol to North Ossetia
⑥ lost by Kabarda-Balkar

——— present-day borders of autonomous republics

– – – old borders and borders of autonomous regions
    and Abkhazian border with Georgia

===== border between Russian Federation and
    Transcaucasus

North Caucasus Territorial Divisions

and Border Changes (1939 - 1991)

Prior to World War II, the city's population was predominantly Polish and Jewish, with a mixture of Belarusians, Russians, Tatars, and even Karaim (a Jewish sect of Turkic origin). Most of the city's Lithuanians became polonized through the centuries of Polish rule, and those who still spoke Lithuanian were not very numerous. The rural population around the city was Lithuanian in the west, Belarusian in the east, and Polish in the south and southwest.

Awarded to Lithuania after World War I, the Wilno region was taken by Polish troops in 1920 and, after a period of transition (during which it was known as "Central Lithuania"), annexed to Poland. When Poland collapsed under Nazi attack in 1939, Stalin gave Wilno to Lithuania, only to swallow them both a year later.

Wilno's Jews were exterminated during the Nazi occupation. After the war, with the city returned to Lithuania under Soviet control, the bulk of the Polish intelligentsia departed for Poland. Those Poles who remained were treated as second-class citizens: use of the Polish language was curtailed, Polish street names were removed, Polish cultural institutions closed, and Poles discriminated against in hirings and promotions. Lithuanian, Russian, and Belarusian newcomers arrived in great numbers.

Today, old Wilno-born families are a small minority in the city. Lithuanians now predominate, followed by Poles and Russians. The small Jewish community is composed of newcomers, with no more than two or three dozen Jewish old-timers still around.

Between 1989 and September 1991, in a sudden reversal of the prior neglect, the Poles of Vilnius were courted both by Soviet central authorities and by the Lithuanian independence movement. The Soviet side raised the odd idea of a Polish Soviet Republic within the borders of the old "Central Lithuania." The Lithuanians sought Polish support for their independence movement with promises of full equality and respect, and Poland's Lech Walesa actively supported Lithuanian independence. The Polish community of Vilnius was divided on the issue: the pro-

The following labels appear on the map:

cities with large
Russian majority

Baltic
Sea

Tallinn

Narva

Kohtla
Järva

Rakvere

annexed by Russia in
1940

Huumaa

ESTONIA

Lake
Peipus

Saarema

Pärnu

Tartu

Ventspils

Riga

LATVIA

Liepaja

Palanga

Daugavpils

Memel (Klaipeda)

Memel
(Klaipeda region)
German to end of
WWII and 1939 - 1944

LITHUANIA

Panevezys

Kaunas

Vilnius (Wilno)

KÖNIGSBERG
(Kaliningrad)

BELARUS

POLAND

Northern East Prussia,
from Germany to
USSR-Russia 1945.

Vilnius (Wilno) region,
(Polish 1920 - 1939)

The Baltic States and
the Königsberg (Kaliningrad) Region

gressives sided with the Lithuanian cause, while others, still holding a grudge against the Lithuanians, were attracted by Soviet inducements.

Another claim to the area was advanced by the Soviet side through the intermediary of Belarusian conservatives: the claim was based on the fact that the Grand Duchy of Lithuania was a Lithuanian-Belarusian state, and that Vilnius (Vilna) had been a Belarusian cultural center as well. This construction had little appeal, since Belarusian presence in Vilnius is currently very limited. During this period the city did harbor Belarusian activists, who enjoyed Lithuanian support.

Soviet conservatives also threatened to contest another area of Lithuania, the Klaipeda (Memel) region. Memel had been in German (Prussian) hands since the Middle Ages. It was Lithuanian between the two world wars, retaken by Hitler in 1939, and returned to Lithuania by Stalin after World War II. The Soviet territorial claims against Lithuania were thus based on the fact that pre-1939 Lithuania included neither Klaipeda, just snatched by Hitler, nor Vilnius, then in Polish hands. Certainly, the importance of the Klaipeda harbor to the military, and the obvious desire to upset the Lithuanian drive toward independence played a role as well. However, the September 1991 recognition of Lithuanian independence by the USSR mentions no territorial claims.

Northeastern Estonia: Soviet claims to the northeastern part of Estonia were presented not directly by the Kremlin, but by the anti-independence "interfront," with its Russian clientele. Devoid of historical basis, the interfront claims were exclusively ethno-demographic: this area, devastated during World War II, had become progressively russified as a consequence of the constant influx of Russian workers hired by newly built factories. Except in the countryside, the percentage of Estonians in the area was small. Interfront forces threatened, in the event that Estonia managed to regain its independence, either to join the Leningrad region or to create an artificial "Estonian" Soviet Republic in opposition to the Republic of Estonia, depriving the latter of a third of its territory. Boris Yeltsin's Russian government endorsed no such claims, and in bilateral treaties recognized the integrity of each republic; but the issue has been kept alive by Russian extremist "red-brown" forces.

In September 1991, Gorbachev, chastened by his August experience, accepted the independence of Estonia without any claims against Estonia's territorial integrity.

Moldova: Border disputes in Moldavia (Moldova) are intricately connected with the Soviet annexation of Romanian Bessarabia in 1940, another consequence of the Soviet-German Non-Aggression Pact of 1939. Bessarabia, in Russian hands since the time of Napoleon, but lost to Romania after World War I, was divided up by Stalin in 1940: the southern and northern extremities were attached to Ukraine, while the rest of the province was added to the small Transnistrian Moldavian Autonomous Republic, which had been created within Ukraine in 1924 on the eastern side of the Dniester River. The combined unit received the status of a union republic. Within Moldova, the demographic situation is different on each side of the Dniester River: on the western side the population is predominantly Moldavian (i.e., Romanian), with a Gagauz minority in the southeast; the eastern side of the river is predominantly Ukrainian and Russian. The "Jewish problem," formerly of importance, was "solved" by Hitler and by the massive outmigration of most of the survivors.

When Moldova moved toward self-determination, the Kremlin repeated its Vilnius tactic by encouraging Ukrainian and Gagauz opposition. The Gágauz (Turkic-speaking Orthodox Christians) formed their own "Soviet Republic," while Russians and Ukrainians established a "Transnistrian Republic" in the area where they constitute a majority. Both "republics" spoke of merging into a "Soviet Moldavia" if the Moldavian Republic (Moldova) opted for Romanian ties.

Since Moldavians are not a nation by themselves, but rather a part of the Romanian nation (which was founded by the merger

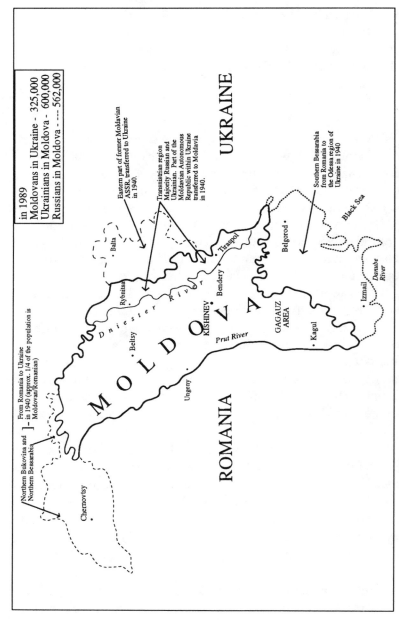

Moldova (Central Bessarabia and Transnistria)

in 1989
Moldovans in Ukraine - 325,000
Ukrainians in Moldova - 600,000
Russians in Moldova - --- 562,000

Eastern part of former Moldavian ASSR, transferred to Ukraine in 1940.

Transnistrian region. Majority Russian and Ukrainian. Part of the Moldavian Autonomous Republic within Ukraine transferred to Moldavia in 1940.

Southern Bessarabia from Romania to the Odessa region of Ukraine in 1940

Northern Bukovina and Northern Bessarabia

From Romania to Ukraine in 1940 (approx. 1/4 of the population is Moldovan/Romanian)

UKRAINE

ROMANIA

MOLDOVA

KISHINEV

Dniester River

Prut River

Danube River

Black Sea

Chernovtsy

Balta

Rybnitsa

Beltsy

Ungeny

Bendery

Tiraspol

GAGAUZ AREA

Belgorod

Kagul

Izmail

of two principalities, Wallachia and Moldavia, the eastern part of which is known under the name Bessarabia), and the Dniester River was in the interwar period the border between Romania and the USSR, it is quite possible that history may repeat itself. In that case the Transnistrian part would rejoin Ukraine, while Bessarabia (the bulk of today's Moldova) would seek ties with Romania. But the fate of southern Bessarabia and of southern Bukovina, incorporated into Ukraine since 1940, would present a problem.

Russia and Ukraine: Russian claims to eastern and southeastern Ukraine have a long history. While Ukrainian lands located within the sixteenth-century borders of the Polish-Lithuanian state are uncontestably Ukrainian, the areas taken from the Khanate of Crimea or as result of the Russian drive toward the Caucasus present a separate problem. They have a large concentration of Russians and are historically connected to both Russia and Ukraine. These areas were never part of the Polish Commonwealth and, consequently, were never subjected to Latin culture and tradition. Perhaps as a consequence, there is much less nationalist feeling among eastern Ukrainians. Fortunately, Russian President Boris Yeltsin has avoided confrontation and has not threatened to dispute the ownership of the eastern and southeastern third of Ukraine.

Fergana: The situation in the Fergana valley originates from the national delimitation of 1925–26 in Central Asia, when the unity of that area was violated. The valley—for centuries the heart of the Khanate of Kokand, and then, after the Russian conquest, a part of the general governorship of Turkestan—was divided among three newly created state units: Uzbekistan, Kirgizia (Kyrgyzstan), and Tajikistan. Initially, only the first was a union republic while the two others were autonomous republics (Tajikistan within Uzbekistan, and Kirgizia within the RSFSR); they were later granted union republic status. The new borders cut across the Fergana valley countryside, disregarding historical ties

from Poland
in 1939

BELARUS

POLAND

from Poland
in 1939
(Austro-Hungarian
from 18th century
to 1918)

Wolyn

Chernobyl

• Rovno

KIEV•

Dnieper River

• Lviv

SLOVAKIA

E. Galicia

• Vinnitsa

•Uzhgorod

Right Bank
Ukraine

HUNGARY

Chernovtsy •

Transcárpathian
Rus
(from Czecho-
slovakia in 1946)

Northern Bukovina
(from Romania in 1940)

MOLDOVA

ROMANIA

Odessa

Transnistrian Moldova
(majority Russian and
Ukrainian)

Southern Bessarabia
(from Romania in 1940)

The Making of

Present-Day Ukraine

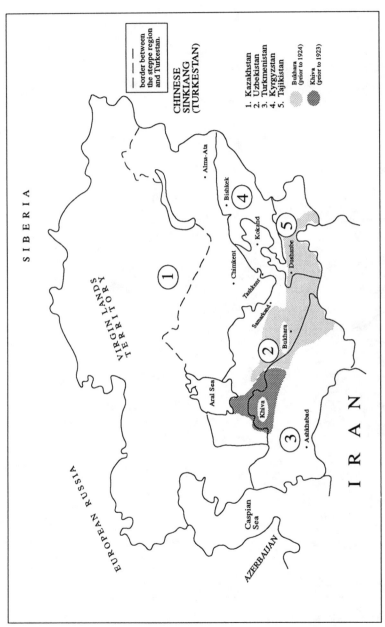

Border Shifts in Central Asia

and ignoring economic realities. Only the ethnic make-up of the area was taken into account. But even the latter criterion was imperfect, given the dense mixture of groups in many localities and the demographic changes that would occur over the next decades. Overpopulation, population shifts, and ecological problems intensified ethnic tensions, leading (during Gorbachev's era) to interethnic violence. The problem is that the valley of Fergana is an indivisible unit, and no "just" borders can be conceived for the three nations sharing the area. Unless the spirit of supranational unity prevails (in the post-Soviet period this probably means pan-Islamic), the problem of state borders in the Fergana valley will remain insoluble.

Other Conflict Points in Central Asia: The Uzbek-Tajik border is a potential source of contention, where the border cuts across the old Emirate of Bukhara. Many urban centers, such as Samarkand and Bukhara, contain a large Tajik population and were long under Tajik (Iranian) cultural influence. But the national delimitation attributed these urban centers to Uzbekistan on the basis of the ethnic composition of the countryside. Despite the current awakening of national feelings among the Tajik city-dwellers of Uzbekistan (who for years listed themselves as Uzbeks in census counts), total numbers favor Uzbekistan, with twenty million inhabitants as against four million in Tajikistan.

The so-called Virgin Lands of northern Kazakhstan, with a large population of settlers, are a possible bone of contention between Kazakhstan and the Russian Republic. This historically Kazakh, but geographically almost Siberian, and overwhelmingly Russian-populated territory is situated to the north of the "hungry steppe," the traditional northern border of Central Asia proper. Aleksandr Solzhenitsyn considered the region part of the Slavic homeland to be retained after jettisoning all Muslim lands. If Kazakhstan joins the rest of Central Asia in a restored Muslim *umma*, the area will undoubtedly be claimed by Russia.

The problem with the inter-republican borders of the former USSR is that for decades they were losing their importance, only to regain it with a vengeance in the late 1980s, when nationalism became resurgent in the republics. As soon as those borders became reality, contestations arose and conflicts developed. When the African states gained independence from colonial rule, they accepted the borders left from European domination, even when those borders cut through tribal lands, as preferable to bloody conflicts aimed at restoring "justice." Boris Yeltsin has obviously been thinking along the same lines. He has accepted the inviolability of established borders in all the bilateral treaties Russia has signed with other republics, even when current borders are not to Russia's advantage. With the old Union no longer in existence, the principle of inviolability of republican borders becomes the essential condition for avoiding the Yugoslav scenario.

3

Language Policies

Language policies in the USSR went through several stages, initially favoring the national languages, then giving priority to Russian, and finally struggling to strike a balance between the two.

At the outset of the Soviet regime, the tsarist policy of dominance of the Russian language and the exclusive use of Russian in all official milieus in non-Russian provinces was reversed. Local languages, even small ones, began to be protected and encouraged and their usage favored in their own republics. In the mid-1920s this policy was pushed even further: Russian-speaking officials in the national republics were required to learn local languages in order to keep their jobs. This policy of *korenizatsiia* (nativization) was welcomed by the non-Russians, but often resented by local Russians. With the end of the 1920s, *korenizatsiia* was stopped, and a compromise was found on the basis of compulsory study of the language of the titular nationality in local educational institutions. State employees, however, were no longer required to speak the local language in official places frequented by the public (from local administrations to post offices).

Unfortunately, Russian students often considered the learning of local languages superfluous, and school authorities failed to exercise the needed pressure to overcome this reluctance.

As far as alphabets are concerned, many small Siberian languages were for the first time provided with a written form (normally based on a Cyrillic alphabet), while the alphabets of all the Turkic or Iranian languages of the country were shifted first from Arabic to Latin, and then from Latin to Cyrillic. The first shift had an antireligious basis; the second favored russification, since the study of Russian was supposed to be facilitated by the similarity of alphabets. The trend today is for adoption of the Latin alphabet used by Turkey.

The process of Russian language learning by non-Russians sometimes produced unfortunate side-effects: many persons never learned more than pidgin Russian, but at the same time their command of their own language was impoverished. This was often the case with the less educated among Ukrainians and Belarusians, whose languages are close enough to Russian to allow easy confusion.

With the coming to power of Nikita Khrushchev, the study of local languages underwent further depreciation; the subject became an elective in schools with Russian as language of instruction, further diminishing the likelihood that Russian children would learn the language of the republic where they lived.

By the time Gorbachev came to power, the non-Russian languages of the USSR were in a state of neglect. Office work was almost exclusively conducted in Russian, except in some areas where there were no Russian residents. Belarusian language instruction was dying, and even Ukrainian was on a speedy decline. In the Baltic republics the local languages held their own, despite being pushed out of public places. Georgians and Armenians were probably the most successful in defending the use of their languages, while many minor tongues were in the process of disappearing. All over the country academic conferences were held on the best way to speed the study and encourage the use of Russian, stressing its value and importance. Russian was said to be the language of "interethnic communication," a must for every Soviet citizen.

Arguments in favor of Russian as the dominant tongue were

many: it was the language of the largest nationality, the language of Lenin and of the October Revolution. It was argued that every multinational state has a principal language of communication— whether English in the United States, German in the old Austro-Hungarian empire, or Turkish in the old Ottoman empire. Russian was supposed to be the language of socialism, while English was that of capitalism and French that of feudalism.

The revival of national self-assertion in the republics started precisely around the issue of national languages. In Ukraine and in Belarus it was the revival of native language education and the use of native tongues in cultural programs on television and radio and at conferences, congresses, and meetings. In the Baltic states the revival went much further: newly elected pro-independence activists enacted an array of laws making the titular language official and directing all public employees to be able to do their work in the language of the republic.

For its part, Moscow saw language demands as less dangerous than other national issues, and was willing to be accommodating in this area.

It should also be mentioned that when the USSR ended its isolation, a new language made its entry into the arena: English, the language of international communication. In many republics (especially, but not exclusively, in the Baltic), even before independence, English was on the way to becoming the key second language. During many international encounters, Baltic and other participants from the USSR ignored Russian and turned straight to English.

Today, the revival of local languages is an accomplished fact, and English is moving into the position it occupies in the rest of the world. Russian is giving way in this competition, but still serves as a *lingua franca*, even among those who dislike it for political reasons. But Russian is also gaining, although in a different way: now that the Russian media are free from the "wooden tongue" mandated under Stalin, the traditional literary beauty of Russian is being restored, an ample reward for its political eclipse.

4

Reinterpreting History

During the Soviet period, the history of the peoples of the USSR was periodically rewritten to suit changing political demands. Thus, at the outset of the Soviet regime, Russian colonial expansion was condemned and the national resistance struggles against tsarist Russian armies were glamorized. The "feudal" and "bourgeois" past of all the nations, and especially of Russia itself, was derided. The historical role of both individuals and states was minimized while the social history of the masses emphasized. The leading proponent of the new approach was the Russian historian Mikhail Pokrovskii, who had developed his revisionist views of history prior to the October Revolution.

In the mid-1930s, as Stalin tightened his grip on the country, a substantial reinterpretation of history took place. The national struggle against Russian colonization was no longer celebrated; instead, Russian expansion was now presented as a "lesser evil" than Turkish, Iranian, or Polish domination or colonial conquest by other European powers. Russia's revolutionary destiny, as well as the nondiscriminatory, egalitarian tendencies supposedly characteristic of the Russian people, was cited in support of such claims. This "rehabilitation" of Great Russia was carried still further in the 1940s in the cause of mobilizing Russian patriotic sentiment against the Nazi invader. Russian tsars and princes, builders and defenders of the empire, were glorified. Prince

Aleksandr Nevskii, Prince Pozharskii, Tsar Ivan the Terrible, Tsar Peter the Great, and princes Suvorov and Kutuzov were hoisted back on to pedestals, while fighters against Russian colonial expansion were speedily demoted and then portrayed as agents of foreign powers.

After Stalin's death, this condemnation of all resistance to tsarist colonial expansion was gradually diluted in favor of a more benign interpretation: nationalist heroes were depicted not as foreign agents but as confused patriots who mistakenly took to arms against the Russians because they failed to realize the advantage of being "liberated," especially in view of all the future benefits Russia could offer.

But even these distorted versions of national histories received little attention in the school curricula. Uzbek, Ukrainian, and Georgian children were supposed to learn Russian history as their own, the way African children in French colonies read about "our ancestors, the Gauls." The official histories of the USSR used in secondary schools and even in higher education focused on the history of Russia, with some information about the republics clumsily appended. These skimpy local accounts were devoted to the topic of class struggle and "liberation" by Russia. If some national feats of arms were lauded, they were directed against other powers (the Poles or the Chinese, for example) or against local landowners (thus Belarusian revolts against Russian domination were presented as class struggles).

An emphasis on Russian military glory was spurred by the experience of World War II. Much to the discomfort of non-Russian soldiers, the old ranks and insignias were revived, along with medals bearing the names of tsarist-era military heroes (including Bohdan Khmelnytsky, the seventeenth-century Ukrainian hetman who brought Ukraine into the Russian fold).

During the period of perestroika, the restoration of the national past to its due place became an essential part of national revival in the republics. Again, as in the case of national language policy, the Kremlin had more important problems on its agenda than censoring history books, and new interpretations began to reach the public. This time, the bias was reversed: local feats were blown out of proportion, Russia's role was ignored or condemned, and regional animosities were resurrected. Sampling some new Armenian and Azeri historical writings—especially their accounts of each other and their respective claims to Nagorno-Karabakh—is enough to give the reader a sharp awareness of the current deformation of history. And these are not exceptions. Russian and Ukrainian writings dealing with the old Kievan Rus are equally biased: Russians overstress the ancient unity of the eastern Slavs, while Ukrainians present Ukraine as the sole heir to old Kiev and depict Russians as a mongrel mixture of Slavic, Finnic, and Tatar strains. The treatment of Bohdan Khmelnytsky and of the "traitor" Mazepa in Russian and Ukrainian histories differs along the same lines. When it comes to Russia's annexation of Belarus, Muscovite historians speak of "reunification" while today's Belarusian writers describe a bloody conquest. The latter celebrate the key position the Belarusian language and culture played in the old Grand Duchy of Lithuania, in the process managing to downgrade the role of Polish and even of Lithuanian contributions. Lithuanian historical writings tend to minimize the role of Poland, whose fate was for centuries connected with that of Lithuania. Estonians and Latvians stress their interwar independence rather than the centuries of foreign rule.

Central Asian historians now seek strength in their long-neglected past, but play down the centuries of stagnation prior to the Russian conquest—precisely the reason for the easy fall of the Central Asian khanates into Russian hands.

Russian history is also being revised. Revolutionary figures are now vilified and long-vilified figures are glamorized. Alexander II, presented as the "tsar-liberator" of the serfs in prerevolutionary histories but smeared during the Soviet period, has regained his old status. Nicholas II, the villain of postrevolutionary writings, now appears as an unfortunate martyr felled by the revolutionary terror. Some Russian chauvinist writers blame revolutionary excesses, and even the revolution itself, on non-

Russians, and especially on Jews. Russia's many troubles in the past and in the present are all attributed to outsiders—foreigners, Masons, Jews and other non-Russians, and foreign powers. Russia is declared to have an imperial destiny, while at the same time it is depicted as being shamelessly exploited by everyone around.

Restoration of truth in history is not easy. It will take some time before objectivity prevails.

5

The Semiotics of Nationality Policies

From the first, the Soviet regime attached a great deal of importance to slogans, catchwords, and codewords. Initially they tended
to reflect real intent, but soon the gaps between labels and reality
grew wider, and the labels acquired new meanings.

Among the initial terms of nationality relations in the USSR
were such formulas as "friendship of peoples," "brotherhood of
peoples," "proletarian unity," and "class solidarity," all express-
ing the purported absence of conflicts between nationalities living under a socialist regime. Newspaper columns celebrated the
internationalist qualities of the proletariat and their unified struggle against the ruling classes of all nations and nationalities.
Class struggle was to replace national struggle. The new proletarian fatherland was not to be affected by national problems. "Yes,
we have Jews, but no Jewish problem" was the classic answer
given by Ostap Bender, a character in the satirical novels by Ilf
and Petrov in the late 1920s and early 1930s.

The dissipation of ethnic conflicts was taken for granted.
Under socialist conditions, nations were supposed to "flourish"
and then grow "closer together" in a process called *sblizhenie*
(rapprochement). The final stage of merger of nations (*sliianie*)
was to be reached once communism triumphed worldwide; states
would "wither away," national differences would disappear along

138

with classes, and money would no longer be needed, since every individual would receive "according to his needs."

In the dialogue between the republics and the center, "flourishing" and "rapprochement" acquired new meanings. The first signified the continuation of autonomous development (of culture, language, and traditions, even if modified by Soviet reality), the second meant progress toward integration. But gradually, the term "rapprochement" was used to suggest not horizontal integration of all the nations of the country but rather absorption of all into Russian culture. The confusion between "Soviet" and "Russian" became increasingly pronounced after World War II, when Stalin proclaimed the Russians to be (if one uses Orwellian terms) "more equal than others." This elevation of Russians into *primus inter pares* was accompanied by the attribution of the qualifier "Great" to the Russian people. For political reasons, some foreign nations (including the Chinese and the Americans) were at times granted the same qualifier, only to have it withdrawn when relations deteriorated.

Stalin himself liked to be called "the father of peoples" (*otets narodov*)—even of those he condemned and deported. On Stalin's orders all the Soviet republics were provided with anthems, shields, and flags of their own, but these had little to do with their past symbols, history, or traditions. Every anthem, except for the Georgian, contained one or more references to the "Great Russian people," and all mentioned Lenin and the October Revolution. Red was the predominant color on each flag, although marginal use of two or three other colors was allowed. Each republic could play with this limited variation. Thus Latvia (after its annexation) was granted little sea waves at the bottom of its flag, and Azerbaijan's had a small oil well. All shields were supposed to bear the inscription "Proletarians of all countries, unite" in Russian and in the language of the titular nationality of the republic. By exception, the original shield of the Belorussian SSR had the same inscription in four languages, adding Polish and Yiddish, a peculiarity eliminated after World War II.

After Stalin's death, the language of nationality policy remained basically unchanged, but the codewords "flourishing," "rapprochement," and "merger" received new treatment. Thus during the Brezhnev years, "rapprochement" was broken down into several stages by the addition of qualifiers, each signifying a degree of progress on the road to eventual merger, giving the illusion that a next stage had been reached. This illusion fit quite well the interests of the leaders of most union republics, who were relieved to see the terminology of nationalities relations anchored at the "rapprochement" level.

In the 1970s the term "merger" began to vanish. It was replaced by the less radical codeword "unity," which was itself soon subjected to the addition of appropriate qualifiers ("full unity," "unshakable unity," etc.). Again a battle of codewords took place, with republican leaders clearly preferring the term *edinenie* (process of unification) over *edinstvo* (unity).

The arrival of Gorbachev had an immediate impact on nationalities terminology. The term *obshchnost* (community of interests), replaced "unity" and "rapprochement" and became a goal in itself, not a stage on the road to a nebulous merger, even in a "historical perspective." But the new term soon became outdated. As power shifted increasingly to the periphery, the republics began to discard the notion of "relative sovereignty" for that of "full sovereignty," and the "flourishing–rapprochement–merger" trio collapsed altogether.

The terminology of nationalities relations during this last period reflected not central pressure and republican resistance, but the republics' drive toward independence and the center's attempt to maintain the status quo. The center initially argued that "full sovereignty" did not imply "independence," then gave in, but insisted that independence in a federal state can be relative, and that the power of both the republics and the center could be strengthened at the same time.

The independence-minded forces in the republics saw sovereignty as absolute. They argued that the federal center enjoyed only the prerogatives conceded by the republics, which could be withdrawn at will. Paradoxically, conservative Russian forces in the non-Russian republics, who alleged persecution by the native majority, began to complain of human rights violations.

During the Gorbachev years, the pretense that nationality problems had been solved was totally dropped, even by the most ardent supporters of the collapsing empire. Codewords denoting imaginary stages on the road to a future utopia gave way to arguments in favor of or against maintaining the Union.

The Union treaty, dating from 1924, was seen as a tight federal contract by the center, as a confederal arrangement by many republican officials, and as an imperial yoke by independence forces. The collapse of the USSR at the end of 1991 brought about a new term, a "Commonwealth" (*Sodruzhestvo*) of Independent States, patterned on the British Commonwealth of Nations or the European Common Market. At the present time it seems unlikely that the conflicts straining this fragile confederation will be fought out only semantically.

6

Religion and Nationalism

Religion is an important, and sometimes inseparable, part of national heritage and tradition, and religious issues and differences must be taken into account in dealing with nationality relations. In discussing the Soviet case two considerations are particularly worth noting: the capacity of religious faith to survive decades of persecution, and the relatively modest role played, at least until now, by religious differences in growing interethnic conflicts.

The Soviet regime, from the very outset, fought a fierce battle against all religions, attempting to replace them by a common communist faith that offered a "glorious future" on earth to the coming generations, the way religion offers paradise in an afterworld. But despite enormous efforts—use of terror, persecution of clergy, destruction of churches, and unabated atheist propaganda—all the religions in the country managed to survive, and immediately surged forward the moment persecution was lifted.

Initially all religions were treated equally harshly by the Bolsheviks, with no preferential treatment accorded. But as early as the 1920s, for tactical reasons, some religions were spared more than others. Thus, in order to pacify large areas of Central Asia affected by the anticommunist *basmachi* revolt, a few Islamic institutions were again allowed to function and antireligious propaganda was relaxed for a short period. The Armenian church fared even better, managing to retain partial immunity from persecution for practically the duration of the Soviet regime.

When Moscow grabbed eastern Poland (western Ukraine and Belarus) in 1939, the Ukrainian Roman Catholic and Uniate churches were singled out for especially harsh treatment. The Orthodox Church received confiscated Catholic and Uniate church buildings, remainders of church property not directly confiscated by the state. The KGB even helped the Orthodox Church to "persuade" members of the Uniate Church (an Eastern rite that, by contrast to Orthodoxy, accepts the Roman Pope) to "reconvert" to Orthodoxy—that is, if they were stubborn enough to reject atheism.

In 1940, after the Soviet-German Non-Aggression Pact, when mass deportations of Catholics took place—first of Poles, then of Lithuanians—and priests were hunted with special fervor because of their Roman ties and Western orientation, it became obvious that communism hated some religions more than others.

But during the war there was a relaxation of religious repression, benefiting first of all the Russian Orthodox Church and to a lesser degree other established religions. The churches were needed to keep patriotic spirits up. Even the Jewish faith had to be shown more tolerance, since Stalin was courting Jewish support in America. However, at the end of the war and the outset of the Cold War, the Jewish religion lost whatever ground it gained.

The postwar position of the Orthodox Church was peculiar. Churches and monasteries were turned into offices, warehouses, antireligious museums, and so forth. Religion was again condemned as the "opium of the masses," and church attendance for working-age individuals was a risky business. On the other hand, some churches and monasteries still functioned. The clergy were no longer dispatched to camps unless they gave additional offense, but their ranks were heavily infiltrated by KGB agents spying on the church and the faithful. The church hierarchy obediently endorsed the Kremlin's foreign policy initiatives when so required. Thus the Moscow Patriarchate got involved in real-estate quarrels with the Orthodox Church of North America over properties in Jerusalem as well as in wooing Haile Selassie's

Ethiopia, meddling in Greek politics, and trying to influence Russian émigré communities in France and the United States.

In the Muslim republics, "official" mullahs were enrolled in the battle against "unofficial Islam" and Sufi brotherhoods, something they did half-heartedly. Both the authorities and the Muslim clergy were aware of the limits official Islam could not overstep without running the risk of losing all its prestige to the infinitely less cooperative parallel clergy and Sufi brotherhoods. The four Muslim muftis, especially the Grand Mufti of Tashkent, were pressured to serve the Soviet cause in the Middle East, something they did more willingly. In Tashkent, a journal published by the Muslim Religious Directorate, *Muslims of the Soviet East,* was printed in a number of foreign languages, but only in one local one, Uzbek, and this in Arabic script, no longer familiar to most Uzbeks since the 1920s.

Relations between the Vatican and Moscow remained strained until the late 1980s. Suspicion lingered that the KGB had been somehow involved in the attempt on John Paul's II life, and so the church kept the names of newly appointed Lithuanian and Latvian cardinals secret. Judaism, except for very few operating synagogues, was in total bondage, with no rabbinical schools, no kosher facilities, and jail sentences for Hebrew teachers. Equally suppressed were various Protestant sects which appeared in the country during the postwar decades, the exception being the long-established Estonian Lutheran Church, which was seen as not very influential. Religious books of all faiths were taboo: no Bibles, no Korans, no Talmuds, no lives of the saints, no prayer books, and no importation of such literature from abroad was permitted, because it was "not needed."

The post-1985 changes in Soviet life brought an immediate revival of all faiths. Churches, mosques, and synagogues were reopened, prohibitions on religious instruction were lifted, religious literature was allowed to be printed or imported, and church attendance soared. These beneficial changes were, unfortunately, followed by a partial revival of interfaith hostilities, albeit in lesser measure than one might have expected.

The Armenian-Azeri conflict has been aggravated by religious differences. The Catholicos of Armenia gave active support to Armenian fighters, and the Shiite Mufti of Baku has been active on the opposite side. Green flags of Islam appeared on Baku streets and anti-Islamic feelings rose high in Erevan. Still, Azeri nationalists took care not to provoke the Russians, who are Christian Orthodox like the Armenians. Likewise, despite their historical hostility toward the Turks, Armenian leaders were careful not to irritate neighboring Turkey with its obvious pro-Azeri sympathies.

In Central Asia's Fergana valley, people of the same faith have joined battle against each other. The same has happened in Moldova, where the fact that Moldavians, Russians, Ukrainians, and Gagauz are of the Orthodox faith did not seem to ameliorate the conflict. Similarly, the Catholicism of both Lithuanians and Poles did not prevent disagreements between the two communities. The Abkhazians, both Christians and Muslims, fight Christian Georgians; the Georgian-Ossetian conflict appears not to be pacified by common faith; Lithuanian-Belarusian difficulties have not been inflamed by religious difference. Russian Orthodoxy has played no special role in interethnic conflicts involving Russian settlers. In Ukraine, quarrels did arise between Orthodox authorities in Moscow and Kiev around the return of church property, and in western Ukraine around the restitution of Uniate property turned over to the Orthodox Church, but these conflicts have not had wider repercussions.

This scarcity of the religious element in interethnic conflicts does not signify a lack of connection between religion and nationalism. But in the current period of intensive religious revival, the main enemy is still the legacy of communist atheism, something that might, unfortunately, change in the future.

Religion as a political force is on the rise in the former USSR, especially in Russia proper, where it is becoming "politically correct" to seek the church's blessing. The Moscow Patriarch blessed Boris Yeltsin when he was elected to Russia's presidency. Priests have been elected to legislative bodies. What may be ominous is that fascist forces such as Pamiat also parade with crosses, and invoke religious justifications for their actions. Whatever the future may be, religion is back in force, with a political power yet to be measured.

7

Ethnic Cadres Policy

An ethnic cadre, or staffing, policy was a mainstay of Soviet nationalities policies. During the civil war, in the very midst of the "class struggle," it was clear that soldiers of specific nationalities tended to side with one or another camp. Cossacks (of Russian or Ukrainian origin, but historically a separate group) mostly supported the Whites, while many Jews acquired fame as Red commissars. Caucasian mountaineers of the White "Savage Division" fought the Reds. Latvian sharpshooters guarded Lenin himself and staffed the first Cheka units. For some years the leading cadres of the Cheka included significant numbers of Poles (including Cheka leader Felix Dzerzhinskii), Latvians, and Jews, with Russians accounting for no more than half the leadership. This is not to deny the fact that there were Red Cossacks, stirringly portrayed in the novels of Mikhail Sholokhov; that a Socialist Revolutionary named Fanya Kaplan took a shot at Lenin; that most Latvians opted for independence; and that few Poles were proud of "their" "Iron Felix."

The habit of classifying national groups at a given historical moment as either friendly or unfriendly to the "cause" became ingrained in Soviet politics, a policy also influenced by the habit of group labeling, which arose from the "class war" philosophy. One can add another consideration: it was shrewd to use *outsiders* for dirty jobs in a given community. Thus Jewish security men were assigned the job of "dealing" with captive White Guards, while Latvian communists were mustered to pacify unruly Russian sailors (who in turn were used against Ukrainian nationalists). During collectivization, Russian big-city activists were dispatched to Cossack areas to carry out the campaign. In the mid-1940s, when it set up a puppet government in postwar Poland, the Kremlin advised Warsaw to use surviving Jewish intellectuals to carry out the unpopular task of sovietization, only to recommend a decade later (under Khrushchev) that the same men should be blamed for the failures of the Moscow-installed system.

During the Stalin years, the republics were divided into "reliable" and "unreliable" categories, and the first supplied watchdogs for the second. Under the pretext of a lack of native proletarian cadres and in the name of brotherly assistance it became routine to dispatch Russian cadres to non-Russian republics, particularly in Muslim regions. Thus within the Party apparatus, Russians (or their surrogates) were assigned the positions of second secretaries at all levels (except for some rural districts), and were the heads of important departments and of security sections. Within the governmental hierarchy, Russians were appointed as deputies to native officials, and given ministerial positions in key spheres. The military command, security, and communications also remained in Russian hands. Ukrainians and Belarusians were trusted surrogates for Russians outside their own republics, just as, during Stalin's time, Armenians and Georgians enjoyed confidence. Jews played the same role during the early stage, but lost their usefulness once Stalin's idea of "socialism in one country" gained ascendancy over "world revolution." The anticosmopolitan campaign of the early 1950s eliminated the few remaining Jews from all power positions. After Stalin's death, Georgia and Armenia were moved into a kind of in-between category, and were saddled with Russian second secretaries at the republic level, but not below.

At the time of Gorbachev's ascension to power, ethnic cadres policies were still strictly observed in all the Muslim republics, in the Baltics, and in Moldavia. In Georgia and Armenia an intermediate pattern prevailed: the Slavic republics supplied the watchdogs, but outside of key control positions, "affirmative action" policies (to use the American term) were operating. Within each republic the titular nationality was granted priority in hiring and promotion, followed by the Slavs, while other minorities were relegated to last place.

Russian second secretaries and other strategically placed Russian *apparatchiki* were rapidly losing power even prior to the August 1991 putsch. Once the Soviet Union and the CPSU were dissolved, little was left for these cadres to do.

In the governing bodies in Moscow, not many non-Russians remained. There are a few highly visible exceptions. The ill-fated Supreme Soviet chairman Ruslan Khasbulatov, for example, is a Chechen. (Another parliamentary leader, Ramazan Abdulatipov, an Avar, emerged from the fall 1993 crisis unscathed.) Viktor Alksnis, a Latvian, has been a figure of the right. What the three have in common is that their political careers have clearly rested on their ability to present themselves as champions of Russian national interests.

8

The Economics of Separatism

The Soviet economy traditionally operated according to well-established principles: state ownership of the means of production; central planning; priority for the military-industrial complex; fixed prices, salaries, and official currency-exchange rates. Economic performance was judged by quantities produced, not by sales or profits.

Party officials, factory managers, and other privileged categories enjoyed a standard of living well above that of the average citizen—mostly through special access to scarce goods rather than significantly higher salaries. The masses were supposed to make sacrifices for a better future for their grandchildren. Nevertheless, practically free rents, transportation, utilities, medical services, and education, as well as inexpensive food supplies, assured everybody's survival. For those who could pay a premium, kolkhoz markets selling goods from collective farmers' private plots, and underground "black markets" offering short-supply items, were alternatives to official, state-controlled sources of goods and services.

In sum, the poor were protected from hunger, people with moderate incomes enjoyed basic comforts, and beginning in the late 1960s and 1970s, a sort of Soviet middle class began to emerge and accede to the Soviet dream: a single-family apartment, a *dacha*, and a private car.

Table 20

Comparative Standards of Living Prior to Perestroika (1986 data)

Republic	Production of consumer goods per capita (rubles)	Child mortality (per 1,000 births) by age 1	Housing space per capita (sq. meters)
RSFSR	1,052	19.3	15.2
Ukraine	1,133	14.8	16.8
Belorussia	1,550	13.4	16.3
Moldavia	1,264	26.4	16.8
Lithuania	1,993	11.6	17.8
Latvia	2,371	13.0	18.9
Estonia	2,312	16.0	20.3
Georgia	1,056	25.5	17.6
Azerbaijan	635	30.5	10.5
Armenia	1,190	23.6	13.7
Uzbekistan	462	46.2	11.0
Kazakhstan	561	29.0	13.0
Kyrgyzstan	607	38.2	11.3
Tajikistan	489	46.7	8.7
Turkmenistan	312	58.2	10.2

Source: Goskomstat SSSR, *Narodnoe khoziaistvo SSSR za 70 let. Iubileinyi sbornik* (Moscow: Finansy i statistika, 1987), pp. 187, 408, 522.

The citizens of the national republics were subject to the same conditions, give or take some regional differences. Thus the Baltic republics, former eastern Galicia, and, in the Transcaucasus, Armenia and Georgia were generally the most prosperous. These regions had territorial compactness, a better-educated labor force, a residual work ethic, an experience of private endeavor, and a historical tradition favorable to independent development and self-reliance. The Muslim republics had high (though hidden) unemployment, serious environmental damage, colonial-type trade relations with the rest of the country, and (except for Azerbaijan) constant need for subsidies. On the positive side, family life there was more intact; private initiative survived in petty commerce, agriculture, and small crafts; and favorable climatic conditions allowed people to get by with less income than in the harsher north.

The three Slavic republics of Russia, Ukraine, and Belorussia were not uniform. Russian Siberia, the non–black-soil areas of central Russia and Belorussia, the capital cities of Moscow and Leningrad, and the industrial towns of the Volga, the Urals, and western Siberia developed their own problems. The non–black-soil areas, victims of rapid industrialization and Khrushchev's policy of consolidating collective farms, were being depopulated; hastily constructed industrial centers were afflicted by blight and ecological problems. Moscow and Leningrad were flooded with "illegal" newcomers, unable to secure the required residence permits. Ukraine, once the grain basket of Europe, had traded a good part of its former agricultural riches for questionable industrial development, but remained energy short.

This was the basic situation as the Brezhnev years drew to a close, a mixed picture of achievements and shortcomings. But some economists saw a deeper problem: lack of dynamism in the Soviet economy, slow growth, and a failure to come to grips with the high-tech revolution, all papered over by the self-satisfied rhetoric of Brezhnev's "era of stagnation."

Mikhail Gorbachev had higher aspirations for the Soviet economy. Recognizing that the USSR was losing ground to the advanced capitalist countries, he resolved to move the Soviet economy out of stagnation, to improve the quality of production, reward performance, encourage individual initiative, and free state enterprises from excessive central controls.

The history of Gorbachev's effort to restructure the Soviet economy—the program known as perestroika—is a long and complicated one, told better elsewhere. But one aspect of the story that has not received sufficient attention is the way inter-republican conflicts and the struggle between central and local interests hindered reform and hastened the collapse of the Soviet economy, dashing Gorbachev's hopes of directing a controlled, gradual transition to a "socialist market" system in the USSR.

Ironically, it was the very nature of the centrally planned Soviet economy, with its enforced dependence on central coordination and its proscription of horizontal ties, that made the economy, like the Union itself, so vulnerable to collapse in the face of political conflict at the center and ethnic conflict at the periphery. Numerous enterprises saw their sources of financing vanish and their usual suppliers default. As central policy zig-zagged, the links between local factories—mediated by the all-Union ministries in Moscow—became unreliable as each enterprise began to fend for itself. The distribution system broke down.

The substantial economic and cultural differences between the republics as well as growing interethnic strife exacerbated the problem, as did the tug-of-war between Moscow and the republics, culminating in the Kremlin's economic embargo against Lithuania (which only increased that country's determination to regain its independence).

To arrest the outflow of scarce foodstuffs and consumer goods, republics started to create custom checkpoints at their borders in order to interdict illegally exported merchandise. Some autonomous republics and even several regions of the Russian Federation followed that path, "protecting" their own borders against unwanted customers. Proofs of local residence were required, and ration books were distributed. Ukraine printed special coupons which had to be used to effect a purchase in the republic.

Even prior to achieving independence some republics printed their own currency with the aim of replacing the Soviet ruble. Thus Estonia printed kronas, but not did not issue them because of concern that they would collapse along with the ruble, damaging the republic's credibility. Kronas were finally put into circulation in the summer of 1992 and aligned with the German mark (at eight kronas to the mark). Other national currencies are being introduced or planned, even within the Commonwealth of Independent States.

Independence presents a harsh economic challenge to all the republics. By design, their economies are strongly interconnected, with various indispensable items produced only in one or

Table 21

Currencies of Former Soviet Republics
(in Russian rubles, 1 December 1993)

		Official exchange rate (rubles per 1 unit of local currency)[a]	Market rate
Ukrainian	Karbovanets[b]	.035	.05
Belarusian	Ruble	.0222	.025
Moldovan	Ruble	.30	.40
Estonian	Krona	89.08	100
Latvian	Lat	1,996.71	2,000
Lithuanian	Lit	308.28	333
Armenian	Dram	200	
Azerbaijan	Ruble	—	—
Georgian	Coupon	—	.04
Kazakh	Tenge	—	260
Tajik	Ruble	—	—
Kyrgyz	Som	—	130
Uzbek	Ruble	.30	—
Turkmen	Manat	—	570

Source: Adapted from Russian Research Center, Harvard University, *Economic Newsletter,* vol. 17, no. 4 (December 25, 1993), citing *Ekonomicheskaia gazeta.*

[a]In December 1993 the Russian ruble–U.S. dollar exchange rate was roughly 1,200 rubles to the dollar.

[b]When first issued, the Ukrainian karbovanets was on a par with the ruble; in December 1993 one ruble was worth 2,000 karbovanets at the market rate.

another of the republics. Driven by inevitable deficits, they are also prey to the uncertainties of the Russian market, the principal customer and the main supplier of energy and raw materials to practically all the former Soviet republics. Since few of the republics' manufactured goods are of adequate quality to be salable on world markets, cutting off traditional customers while searching for Western clients is a dangerous game.

The demise of the Union, however, has unquestionably projected the former republics in separate directions. The Baltic states are knocking on the doors of the Nordic countries. Ukraine and Belarus look westward to their Slavic neighbors, Poland and the Czech Republic, but have resisted economic reform at home. Moldova, whose Romanian connection cannot deliver much, is enmeshed in a civil war in Transnistria, which threatens its relations with Russia and Ukraine. The Central Asian republics and Azerbaijan have moved to develop closer ties with Turkey and other countries of the region, but seek Western investments as well. Armenia, entangled in the war over Nagorno-Karabakh and subjected to an economic blockade by Azerbaijan, is sustained by its diaspora. Georgia is just beginning to emerge from isolation in a quest for support in the struggle to survive its many internal wars.

By the end of 1992, economic hardships were fueling political crises in several former Soviet republics, including Russia itself. The lifting of price controls coupled with the breakdown of old inter-republican supply networks caused tremendous problems. Employees of state enterprises and retirees living on small pensions found themselves sinking below the poverty level. The cheapening of money as a consequence of rapid inflation, and rising prices, not only in ruble terms but in hard currency as well, accelerated the process of pauperization. Among those who managed to stay afloat and even prosper under the new circumstances were the same old well-connected apparatchiks, the established black-marketeers, and the fast-developing mafias (most often based in common ethnic or regional ties). The new generation is better able to adapt to the new circumstances, but even young businessmen are forced to pay heavy tribute to increasingly corrupt officials and voracious protection rings. The rise of criminality, along with signs of serious political instability and resistance to any further economic reform that would result in closures of state-subsidized enterprises, did much to cool the enthusiasm of foreign firms for investment in Russia as well as other new states.

Under pressure from Russia's parliament, President Boris Yeltsin was forced to demote his acting prime minister, Egor Gaidar, an avid free marketeer, for a more moderate nominee; but this brought only a short reprieve. The December 1993 parliamentary elections, held in the wake of the bloody confrontation with Yeltsin's opponents at the Russian "White House,"

Table 22

Income Groups in the Russian Federation
(September 1992 data per family)

Income group	Income in rubles (000)	% spent on food	% of population
(1)	under 3.5	appx. 100	33–37
(2)	3.5–10.0	70–80	33–35
(3)	10.0–45.0	38–42	18–20
(4)	over 45.0[a]	10–25	13–15

Source: Argumenty i fakty, 1992, no. 35 (September 1992).
[a]Approximately 2.3–2.7 percent of families had income in excess of 100,000 rubles.

showed the strength that both "red" and "brown" opponents of reform were able to command.

The picture that emerges is alarming. The reality of economic interdependence clashes with nationalist fervor, complicating the enormous task of economic transition. The future appears hazy at best, with few prospective winners and many losers in the short run.

Part 4

Policies

1

The Marxist Approach to Nationality Problems

The nineteenth century saw the rise of national consciousness all over Europe. Napoleonic armies carried the free spirit of the French Revolution across the continent, awakening the hopes of oppressed nationalities as well as the dormant nationalism of the countries that were fighting the French.

The industrial revolution of the second part of the century, on the other hand, gave birth to socialist theories based on the primacy of social issues over national considerations. Marx, Engels, and their followers saw the modern world as a single society dominated by capitalism, and believed that class warfare would supersede national struggles. The internationalist spirit of the Paris Commune reinforced their view that nations and national differences would lose all importance upon the triumph of the socialist revolution. In the name of "international proletarian solidarity," a class-conscious worker would see his "fellow workers" across the border as "comrades" and the "bourgeoisie" everywhere as the enemy. Nationalism was a dangerous distraction from this primary class loyalty. Accordingly, Engels viewed the assimilation and disappearance of small nations in positive terms.

The test of German Marxist theories came during World War I, when socialist parties in the belligerent countries sided with their own governments; international workers' solidarity surfaced only sporadically. For the most part, national solidarity prevailed and was even reinforced by the war—as would prove true again during the Polish defense of Warsaw against the advancing Red Armies.

Many prerevolutionary Russian Marxists saw the Russian empire as, in Lenin's words, a "prison of peoples," but believed that the socialist revolution would automatically solve the problem by ending the exploitation of the weak by the strong. But other socialist parties took different positions on the question. Among Russian revolutionary parties, the Socialist Revolutionaries were the first to recognize, albeit only theoretically, the right of nations to self-determination, but they did this with serious reservations.

The members of the Jewish Bund advocated "extraterritorial" cultural autonomy for the Jewish population. The Bundist view was based on ideas developed by the Austrian Marxist Otto Bauer. Given the entangled multinational character of many parts of the Habsburg empire, Bauer believed that the best solution was to recognize the national-cultural rights of all groups, whether they lived in a specific territory or not. This conception disapproved of nationalism and endorsed "international solidarity" while advocating equal rights for all nationalities and "cultural autonomy" for "a people of one nationality spread throughout the country." By contrast, Jewish Bolsheviks (and even Mensheviks) tended to see Jewishness as a religious rather than a national identity. They perceived the "Jewish question" purely in terms of discrimination, something that would automatically disappear (along with the religion as such) after the revolution.

Among revolutionary groups in the Caucasus, the widely dispersed Armenians were ready to endorse Bundist theories, but most others were looking for political autonomy based on territorial principles (i.e., as the entitlement of a specific nation residing within its own historical borders).

When nationality problems barged uninvited onto the Russian Marxists' political agenda, the Bolsheviks commissioned a young Georgian, Iosif Djugashvili (Stalin), to tackle the subject.

In his work known as *Marxism and Nationalities*, published in 1913, Stalin fulfilled his assignment, putting on paper his own definition of a nation, based on four criteria: community of language, territory, economic life, and psychological make-up (culture). At that time Stalin accepted that "every oppressed nation should be free to break away from Russia." His view became the basis for the most important right granted to each union republic in the postrevolutionary USSR. However, after the success of the revolution, Stalin found a way to qualify his prerevolutionary generosity, specifying that: "The principle of self-determination ought to be understood as the right of self-determination not of the bourgeoisie, but of the toiling masses of a given nation."

While Stalin moved away from his original position favoring the non-Russian nations, Lenin evolved in the opposite direction. He conceded that, although in a developed country the proletariat should fight the bourgeoisie, in a colony the fight for independence might take precedence, and a national-liberation movement could house an alliance between the proletariat and the more "progressive" part of the local bourgeoisie. In the case of the Russian empire, Lenin finally accepted the right of self-determination of nations, although it was not his preference, using the analogy: "We hardly mean to urge women to divorce their husbands, though we want them to be free to do so."

In 1917 Lenin accepted the right of separation of Poland and Finland from Russia, against the objections of Nikolai Bukharin and Felix Dzerzhinskii, who saw his policy as "a purposeless concession to bourgeois nationalists"—a theme echoed by Stalin, who underscored that "secession is not a solution."

Since the great majority of Russian Marxists gave little thought to nationality issues, and Stalin emerged as the official Bolshevik spokesman on this question, his views laid down the basis for future developments and his retreat from the principle of self-determination would become the keystone of future Soviet policies in this domain.

2

Lenin's Nationality Policy, 1917–1922

Knowledge of the initial period of Soviet nationality policy, a time when Lenin and not Stalin had the decisive voice, is crucial to an understanding of the future discrepancy between the official right of nations to self-determination and the Kremlin's systematic obstruction of the exercise of that right by the nations under its control.

The first major pronouncement of the new revolutionary regime, the Declaration of the Rights of the Peoples of Russia (November 21, 1917), recognized four major principles:

1. Equality and sovereignty of the peoples of the Russian empire;
2. The right of peoples to self-determination to the point of secession;
3. Abolition of all privileges based on nationality or religion;
4. Freedom of cultural development for national minorities (both small nationalities and all those living outside their historic territories).

These were tactical concessions, motivated by the need to attract non-Russian support to the Russian revolutionary cause.

Barely two months later, the Third Congress of Soviets (January 1918) restricted the right of secession to the "toiling masses of a given nation," thus nullifying the main point of the November 1917 declaration. The first Soviet constitution (1918) followed the same pattern. It reserved for "the workers and peasants of each nation" the right to decide "whether they want to take part in the federal government and in other federal institutions." This loophole allowed the center to reject all separatist demands as contrary to the wishes of the masses, whose only legitimate spokesmen were, virtually by definition, those Party functionaries who were pliant to Kremlin directives. Those who persisted on an independence course were swiftly branded nonrepresentative of the people's wishes and accused of treason—an effective deterrent under the increasingly oppressive political conditions of Bolshevik rule.

The events that followed confirmed the direction of Bolshevik policy. Whenever feasible, Moscow fought against self-determination, accepting only the inevitable. In Finland, a tsarist province with a substantial degree of autonomy whose right to independence Lenin acknowledged, Moscow initially recognized both the new independent government and a competing puppet regime backed by Soviet troops. After the military defeat of the latter in 1919, Moscow pursued normal relations with "bourgeois Finland." When the opportunity presented itself twenty years later, Moscow repeated the same scenario, and after it again failed to annex Finland, resumed normal relations once more.

In the case of Poland, Moscow initially saw no possibility of preventing independence. But during the Polish retreat from Kiev in 1920, following an unsuccessful Polish move to restore its eighteenth-century borders, a reintegration of Poland into Moscow's fold was attempted. The advance Soviet forces set up a puppet Polish government under Felix Dzerzhinskii, the Polish-born head of the notorious Cheka. This government, based in occupied Bialystok, was short-lived: Polish troops soon reversed the situation, and pushed eastward past Bialystok. After concluding that the Polish proletariat was not yet ready for revolution, Lenin accepted the Treaty of Riga and surrendered a good chunk of Belarusian and Ukrainian lands to Warsaw. Again, as in the case of Finland, when the opportunity presented itself in 1939, and again in 1944–45, Moscow tried to recover its losses.

In November 1917, a newly established Ukrainian parliament, the Rada, proclaimed its own People's Republic. In response, the new Bolshevik government issued an ultimatum demanding that the Rada recognize the Soviet regime's authority in Ukraine and render assistance to Red Army troops. Faced with the Rada's defiance, Moscow established a competing Ukrainian government based in Kharkov. This dual power lasted for a while, but after the Rada proclaimed full independence for Ukraine in January 1918, Soviet troops marched on Kiev to end the stand-off. When Soviet troops had to relinquish Kiev as a condition of the Brest-Litovsk Treaty by which Russia withdrew from the war with Germany, the Rada was reestablished and the previous scenario was repeated once again. The Soviet Ukrainian government retreated to Kharkov, and after the collapse of German forces in the finale of the World War I, Kiev was taken again. During the civil war, which raged on Ukrainian soil between the Reds and General Denikin's White Armies, Kiev changed hands a few more times, until it was finally secured by Soviet troops in December 1919, ending all dreams of Ukrainian independence. The short-lived Polish occupation of Kiev during the Soviet-Polish War of 1920 failed to revive the independence movement.

The Belarusian scenario was in many ways similar. A Rada established in August 1917, between the February and October revolutions, was overthrown by Soviet forces, then reestablished by the Germans after Brest-Litovsk, and overthrown again in December 1918. A Moscow-backed scheme to create a Belorussian-Lithuanian Federation (spring 1918), as a way of recovering Lithuania, failed to materialize. Finally, in 1920, the Belorussian Soviet Republic was proclaimed as a country of Belorussian, Russian, Polish, and Jewish toilers (symbolized by a shield carrying the words "Proletarians of all countries, unite" in all four languages).

In Latvia and Estonia, Soviet regimes were proclaimed right

after the October Revolution, but failed to survive the nationalist upsurge supported initially by German troops and later by British gunboats. The nationalists were able to consolidate their positions, and Moscow resigned itself to the new reality and signed peace treaties with both republics in 1920.

In Lithuania, a National Council (Tariba) was set up in the winter of 1917–18 under German protection. After the German collapse, a Soviet government was established in Vilnius (Wilno), but the city was soon taken by the Poles. Fifteen months later, when war broke out between Russia and Poland, Soviet troops recaptured the city. Retreating eastward once again, the Soviets turned the city over to the "bourgeois" Lithuanian government based in Kaunas. This was done not out of love for the Lithuanians, but out of a desire to foster Polish-Lithuanian conflict. Poland recovered Wilno by force shortly thereafter and kept it until 1939, when Moscow once more "gave" Vilnius to Lithuania, only to swallow up both Lithuania and the "gift" less than a year later. Nevertheless, in 1920, Lithuania, separated from Soviet Union by a strip of Polish territory, was given a twenty-year lease on life.

In the Transcaucasus, Georgia, Armenia, and Azerbaijan were joined in a Transcaucasian federation, but soon each nation went its own way: a socialist (Menshevik) government took power in Georgia, a nationalist one emerged in Armenia, and a string of regimes appeared in Baku. In 1920 Georgia won recognition from the Western powers and from Moscow, but in February 1921 Soviet troops entered Georgia and established a Soviet regime. Armenian independence was suppressed by Turkish forces, reestablished by the British, then threatened once more by both the Turks and the Soviets.

After British, Turkish, and even Armenian intervention, Soviet troops managed to take hold of Baku (the capital of Azerbaijan and the largest industrial town of Transcaucasus), and then used their Baku base to recover the rest of Transcaucasus.

In Central Asia, after the October Revolution, Russian settlers took control of Tashkent, the capital city of Turkestan, while the former Russian protectorates of Khiva and Bukhara retained their old status and form of government. This situation continued as long as the area was severed from the rest of the country by White forces operating in Siberia and Kazakhstan. A Muslim attempt to form a government in Kokand was easily suppressed, while native participation in the Soviet government in Tashkent was kept to a minimum. But as soon as Russian forces broke through from the north and entered the area, coups were staged in both Khiva (April 1920) and Bukhara (September 1920). The old regimes were overthrown by Red troops aided by local leftists, and the "people's republics" of Khorezm (Khiva) and Bukhara were proclaimed. These republics were the first prototypes of future Soviet satellites elsewhere in the world. In January–March 1921, "national-revolutionary" governments in both people's republics were unseated, and new, more compliant native leaders were chosen by the Tashkent authorities to rule the little satellites.

Muslim resistance, the so-called *basmachi* revolt against the Soviet regime, had been raging in Central Asia since 1918, but despite some successes, it peaked in 1922 and was eventually pacified through a combination of massive repression and the skillful use of local national-communists, who tried to combine nationalism with communism.

The early Soviet nationality policy was remarkable for its great hopes and broken promises, local variations in the policy notwithstanding. The initial proclamation of the right of nations to self-determination was followed almost immediately by measures curtailing that right, justified by the need to protect the interests of the "toiling masses" of the given nation. In some cases the "toiling masses" were specified as workers (factory workers), who were most often Russians. The favored tactic was to back competing "Soviet" governments in opposition to national governments, with the Red Army lending active support. Cooperation with national-communist leaders was usually short-lived as they were eliminated in favor of more obedient, hand-picked successors (some were removed as early as the 1920s, others during the purges of the 1930s).

3

Soviet Nationality Policy
in the 1920s

The period from 1922 (roughly the time when Lenin became incapacitated by illness) to the end of the 1920s was a key formative period for Soviet nationality policies. During that period Stalin was rising to absolute power, but was still tied to Lenin's vision of federalism for the nations of the reconstructed empire, a vision more egalitarian than his own.

The historical interpretation of Russian colonial conquests during that period was influenced by Mikhail Pokrovskii's school of historical interpretation, which condemned all colonization, whether Russian, French, or English, and lauded native resistance. Russian chauvinism was seen as colonial in nature and the past misdeeds of the Romanovs' colonial rule were acknowledged.

Three major elements marked the period in question:

• The first all-Union constitution of 1924 established the legal framework of vertical relationships between the center and the republics, a framework that lasted until August 1991. It gave little attention to horizontal ties between the republics.

• The policy of *korenizatsiia*, or nativization (promotion of national languages and cultures)—a positive development as far as nationalities were concerned, but one that failed to survive into the next decade.

• Establishment of national-territorial units for some nations that had never had them before, and a redrawing of borders. In Central Asia, preexisting states were dissolved and new state units were constructed on their territories, cutting across old borders.

The first all-Union constitution established two legislative chambers. The Soviet of the Union was to represent the population at large according to sheer numbers, while the Soviet of Nationalities was made of delegates from national republics and regions. Each national-territorial unit of equal status was allowed the same number of seats in this chamber, regardless of the size of its population. Union and autonomous republics (the latter being component parts of the former) initially had equal representation (five seats) in the Soviet of Nationalities; each autonomous region was given one seat.

The new constitution established the basic pattern of government ministries (then called people's commissariats). The all-Union ministries at the center got the lion's share of power. Only agriculture, education, health, sanitation, social security, local economy, and internal affairs were left in the hands of the republics (the 1936 constitution would move most of these sectors into the all-Union column). The republics were barred from any direct contacts with foreign powers, whether diplomatic or commercial. Taxation and budgetary matters, communications and transportation, were also removed from republican competence.

Another novelty incorporated in the constitution was the establishment of "enterprises of all-Union importance," directly subordinated to central authorities. This unusual provision later became the centerpiece of Moscow's control over the republics. If at the beginning, only large enterprises were so classified and they were not too numerous, all large new factories built during the following decades joined the ranks, with the result that up to three-quarters of industrial production was under central rather than republican jurisdiction. Moreover, both management and workers in most of these enterprises were predominantly Russians, in effect turning the factories into Russian strongholds on national republican territory. Even the party organizations in such enterprises were subordinated to Moscow, and bypassed the usual ladder of local authority.

On the positive side, the policy of *korenizatsiia* introduced in the 1920s, even though it was reversed in the 1930s, proved to have a long-lasting effect on the development of national relations in the USSR. *Korenizatsiia* consisted of a series of measures taken by individual republics to ensure the development of local languages and cultures that had been suppressed under tsarist rule. Thus, in Ukraine and Belarus, the national languages were made compulsory in schools and offices, books and newspapers were printed in those languages, national theaters were opened, and public employees were required to answer inquiries in Ukrainian and Belarusian.

In Central Asia, the emphasis was more on secularization and access to world culture (as mediated by the party): local alphabets were shifted from Arabic to Latin, as Kemal Ataturk had done in Turkey, and later to Cyrillic. In the North and in Siberia, alphabets were devised for nationalities that had not had a written language before.

Even after it was discontinued, *korenizatsiia* remained the cultural ideal for native intellectuals. During the initial stages of perestroika, the first demands voiced by the national republics were for a return to the principles of *korenizatsiia*.

The reluctance of Russians settlers to learn the languages of the republics where they lived and worked became, with time, a major obstacle to successful interethnic integration, something for which they would pay dearly in the future.

The national delimitation of the mid-1920s was another event that would have far-reaching repercussions. The task entailed a redrawing of borders in Central Asia and Kazakhstan, erasing the old boundaries of Khiva and Bukhara, Turkestan and the Steppe Region. The aim was to create modern national republics in place of feudal formations, and to split the historic unity of Turkestan in order to make the area more manageable. Thus the aim was a double-edged one, with both progressive and neocolonialist implications.

Tracing new borders proved to be an onerous task. It was impossible to follow the ethnic distribution of the population exactly, especially in highly mixed areas. Geographic obstacles, existing economic ties, and conflicting historical claims further complicated the task. The new borders failed to match the ethnic lines or to take into account the ethnic make-up of the urban centers, thus leaving room for future conflicts. Still, the most important result was that over time these newly created national republics lost their artificiality and fostered a feeling of national identity among communities whose allegiance had previously been directed toward religion, local dynasties, and clans. Thus the formation of modern nations started in the 1920s in Central Asia and was achieved a few decades later, when national allegiance proved stronger than either supranational or subnational identities in the breakup of the USSR.

The original national delimitation scheme in Central Asia led to the establishment of two union republics (Uzbekistan and Turkmenistan) as well as three autonomous republics (Tajikistan, Kazakhstan, and Kyrgyzstan) that were later promoted to the higher "rank."

The North Caucasus, in turn, was divided into three autonomous republics within the RSFSR (Chechen-Ingush, Kabarda-Balkar, and North Ossetia), and two autonomous regions (Karachai-Cherkess and Adyge). In addition, the Dagestan ASSR contained a number of different nationalities of linguistically unconnected origin. The shuffling of groups and redrawing of borders created opportunities for new territorial conflicts.

In Siberia, a score of national-territorial units was created, providing indigenous peoples with their own, often unsolicited, "national homes."

However imperfect, national delimitation created the reality of today, gave form to new national-territorial units, and provided them with the modern identity with which they have to live from now on.

4

Stalin's Nationality Policy in the 1930s (1930–1941)

During the 1930s Soviet nationalities policy lost its internationalist coloring. The reality of Stalin's plan for "socialism in one country," discounting the probability of world revolution in the foreseeable future, served to enhance the role of the "leading nation," namely Russia, and to diminish the relative importance of all others. The non-Russians were no longer viewed as possible bridges to the outside world, whether East or West. The conflict between the internationalists (often non-Russians, and frequently Jews) and the Moscow-centrists began with the struggle for power between Stalin and Trotsky. The liquidation of Soviet officers who had "fulfilled their internationalist duty" aiding loyalist forces during the Spanish Civil War was the last episode in that struggle.

The waves of purges during the 1930s, in the wake of collectivization, the mass deportations of kulaks, and the forced settlement of nomadic groups, soon reached the national-communist cadres in every national republic. While the Russians themselves were hit as well, the local cadres of the national republics were often few and fragile, making their decimation a much more severe blow. Thus in the Central Asian republics, almost all local communists of status disappeared, to be replaced by newcomers selected for their obedience to the center and their desire to climb the power ladder. In perhaps a less obvious manner, the same took place in the other republics as well.

At the same time, the anticolonialist views of Mikhail Pokrovskii, which had dominated official histories in the previous decade, were replaced by the depiction of Russian conquest as a lesser evil in comparison with other alternatives. Soon this interpretation was dropped in favor of the idea that Russian domination was an absolute good, an event beneficial to all the conquered nations. Russia was increasingly held up as the "elder brother" whose selfless deeds on behalf of lesser nations dated to prerevolutionary times.

In order to strengthen Russia's influence, the alphabets of all the Turkic nations of the USSR (plus a few others) were shifted to Cyrillic, despite the fact that the previous shift (from Arabic to Latin) had just taken place. The new change was presented as beneficial for two reasons: Cyrillic, with its larger number of letters, was supposedly better suited for Turkic languages; and early learning of the Cyrillic alphabet would facilitate the study of Russian, an obvious necessity for every Soviet citizen. While the second reason had some validity, the first was dubious since the Latin alphabet is used by Turkey and learning it facilitates the study of European languages. (Indeed, the use of Cyrillic had been considered in the 1920s, but rejected as less practical.) Today the alphabets are in process of being shifted back to Latin despite some voices in favor of Arabic script.

A new constitution of the USSR, the so-called "Stalin Constitution," was adopted in 1936. Its importance cannot be overstated, since it lasted until 1977, albeit with numerous amendments. The 1936 constitution expanded national-territorial representation in the Soviet of Nationalities from two levels (republics and autonomous regions) to four, with twenty-five delegates per union republic, eleven per autonomous republic, five for each autonomous region, and one for each autonomous district.

The rights conceded to nationalities in the new constitution

were liberal in appearance but ill-defined. The fundamental provision, carried over from the 1924 constitution, was Article 17:
"The right freely to secede from the USSR is reserved to every
republic." However, this right was not backed by any "how to"
provision, since there was no intention that it would ever be
exercised.

The sovereignty of the republics was to be limited only by the
powers conceded to the federal authorities (Article 15), but those
powers (Article 14) were far wider than in 1924 and left little
under direct republican jurisdiction. Here we see a prime example of Stalin's political approach: to proclaim all sorts of freedoms, but to allow none. Thus we have the freedom to secede
without a corresponding mechanism, sovereignty without jurisdiction, elections without competing candidates, the freedom to
support socialism but not to oppose it, and so forth.

But although the rights granted by the Soviets were paper
rights, the forms were there and the rights were named. It was
only in Gorbachev's time that these empty texts began to come
alive, finally fulfilling their original promises.

The close of the decade saw the complete degradation of the
internationalist ideal in the USSR, when Stalin made an abrupt
shift from antifascism to entente with Hitler, cemented by the
Soviet-German Non-Aggression Pact signed by Molotov and
Ribbentrop in August 1939. The ensuing annexation of western
Ukraine, Belarus, the Baltic states, and Bessarabia signaled the
replacement of the old internationalist hope for revolution in Europe by pure and simple imperialist expansion, cynically cloaked
in internationalist slogans. Russia's past military victories under
empire-builders back to the time of Ivan the Terrible were glamorized, while the histories of other component republics of the
USSR were increasingly treated as minor appendages to Russian
history, as if their most glorious moment was their absorption
into the Russian empire.

By the beginning of the 1940s, all the national republics of the
USSR were headed by Moscow's puppets, trained in unques-

tioned obedience. The terms "Russian" and "Soviet" became increasingly interchangeable, and the old internationalist slogans were merely instruments of Russian imperial interests. The true believers were, by now, either dead or languishing in Siberian camps.

5

Moscow and Nationalities in the 1940s

In the wake of the German attack on the Soviet Union on June 22, 1941, the Kremlin took another step away from the concept of equality among nations. This time the peoples of the USSR were overtly divided by the Kremlin into reliable and unreliable categories, with the latter subject to collective harsh treatment, including deportation (see part 2, chapter 1, on "punished peoples"). This departure from egalitarian principles, justified by accusations of collaboration with the Germans, set a precedent for later condemnation of the Jews (who could not, of course, be accused of such collaboration). The high point of Stalin's anti-Jewish campaign was reached in 1952, just a year before his death, with the announcement of the so-called "doctors' plot," a charge that Jewish physicians had tried to kill Stalin. This was to be a prelude to a mass "voluntary" resettlement of Jews to Birobijan, a course arrested by Stalin's own death.

During the war, draftees of some non-Russian nationalities were directed predominantly to labor units while others were entrusted with the privilege of carrying arms. This division between those who were perceived as "more" or "less" reliable outlasted the war. It affected primarily Muslim draftees, who by 1990 accounted for four out of every ten conscripts in the Soviet army. At the same time, Red Army ranks and insignias were replaced with military decorations bearing the names of tsarist Russian military heroes. In his victory speech at the end of the war, Stalin would laud the special qualities of the Russian people and their role in the defeat of the invader.

In 1944 a new anthem replaced the revolutionary "International," which had been composed by a Frenchman in 1875 to celebrate the fallen Paris Commune and the ideal of international worker solidarity and struggle. The new "Hymn of the Soviet Union" broke with that theme. It glorified not only Russia, but her imperial role as well ("An unshakable union of free republics was forever wrought together by Great Russia"). In the new anthem the national republics appeared not as actors but as passive objects gathered into the Great Russian fold. The new anthem survived until 1991, when the "International" became the official Communist Party song.

Although Stalin's actions in the field of nationalities policy in the 1940s were unremittingly negative, in February 1944 some reforms were introduced which enhanced the appearance of sovereignty of the national republics. The Dumbarton Oaks Conference (August–October 1944), which laid the foundations for the new United Nations organization, provided the incentive. Stalin tried to have all sixteen Soviet republics (then including the so-called Karelo-Finnish Republic) represented in the new organization. The matter was later settled by granting seats to three: the USSR itself, plus the Ukrainian and Belorussian SSRs. The Kremlin allowed the establishment of Ukrainian and Belorussian missions to the United Nations (which became subsidiaries of the Soviet mission) as well as the creation of republican ministries of foreign affairs and of defense, enhancing the illusion of self-government for the union republics. However, the exact competence of the new ministries was never fully defined, and they experienced years of total neglect. For all practical purposes, the republican ministries of foreign affairs turned into state tourist agencies. In time the republics were invited to establish representations in Moscow and were granted buildings to house their offices and to provide lodging for visiting officials. These "missions" in Moscow became lobbying centers for republican interests.

The republican ministries of defense had an even less well defined function. National military units had existed during the revolution but were later abolished. They were revived during World War II in some of the republics, but were terminated soon thereafter. Without any national military units, the republican ministries of defense had few responsibilities other than some civil defense and draftboard matters as well as a token presence at military parades.

6

Khrushchev's Nationality Policies

Khrushchev's era was a time of mixed blessings as far as nationalities were concerned. On the one hand, in line with his de-Stalinization policies, Khrushchev rehabilitated all the nations condemned by Stalin during World War II, freed political prisoners from the camps, and allowed scores of "nationals" to return to their homelands (except for the Volga Germans, Crimean Tatars, and Meskhetian Turks). The national-territorial autonomies of other "punished peoples" were restored, albeit within slightly narrower borders, adjusted in Russia's favor.

While repairing some of Stalin's injustices, Khrushchev toyed with the idea that the borders of the republics had lost their prior significance. Persuaded of the success of Soviet nationality policies, Stalin's transgressions notwithstanding, on several occasions Khrushchev did not hesitate to upset the principle of territorial integrity of the republics.

The February 1954 transfer of the Crimean region of the RSFSR (the former Crimean Tatar ASSR) to Ukraine, a sort of three-hundredth "wedding anniversary gift" from Moscow to Kiev commemorating Bohdan Khmelnytsky's union with Moscow, was almost an echo of medieval times when entire states were part of a queen's dowry in marriage to a neighboring king. In this curious transaction, the deported Crimean Tatars were utterly ignored and the current ethnic composition of the region (majority Russian) was disregarded. The transfer was hailed as a sign of trust in Ukrainian allegiance to the Union (i.e., to Moscow), but the reality was that Khrushchev believed inter-republican borders no longer mattered.

Another interesting case was the establishment of the Virgin Lands Territory (mid-1950s), which encompassed several regions of northern Kazakhstan. Khrushchev had originally entertained the idea of simply detaching that part of Kazakhstan from the republic and attaching it to the RSFSR, but abandoned the project for fear of negative domestic and international reaction. (In 1990, Solzhenitsyn—no admirer of Khrushchev—would advocate the same idea in his pamphlet about reorganizing Russia.) The newly established territory, with its looser ties to Alma-Ata and more direct connection to Moscow, became the recipient of masses of Slavic settlers, whose agricultural experiment resulted in the creation of another dust bowl. In 1965, a year after Khrushchev's fall from power, the territorial unit was abolished and its component regions were returned to the Kazakh republican administration.

In 1956 the Karelo-Finnish SSR, created in 1940 in order to facilitate the planned annexation of Finland, was reduced to its former status as an autonomous republic. While the move was aimed at normalizing relations with neighboring Finland, it created a strange constitutional precedent: a union republic renounced its own sovereignty and reintegrated itself into the RSFSR of its own "free will."

Another of Khrushchev's measures was the establishment of economic regions which did not always coincide with republican borders. Needless to say, this measure did not improve Khrushchev's standing with local authorities.

In 1958, Khrushchev's position on nationality issues took another turn for the worse. Among the first symptoms was a shift of emphasis in theoretical discussions from the theme of the "flourishing" of nationalities to that of their ultimate "merger," a clear signal of weakened commitment to national autonomy. Second, a new education law allowed Russian schools in non-Russian republics to make the study of local languages elective rather than compulsory. Since study of the Russian language was universally required, the exemption of Russians living in the republics from a reciprocal obligation estranged them further from these nations. Opponents of the new law were speedily removed from office.

The revival of the anti-Semitic theme developed by Stalin in the early 1950s (under the guise of anti-Zionism) was another phenomenon of Khrushchev's era. It was probably motivated by a combination of his personal prejudices, foreign policy considerations (the USSR was actively seeking alliances in the Arab Middle East), and growing Jewish participation in the dissident movement. The latter began to gain momentum after Khrushchev wavered in his pursuit of de-Stalinization once he had eradicated the most flagrant abuses.

The fifth paragraph in Soviet internal passports (which lists the bearer's nationality) became increasingly important for admission to schools and universities, hiring, firing, and promotions. In this connection it should be noted that in Eastern Europe nationality and citizenship are not the same; the first defines what in American or West European terms is known as "ethnic origin."

The most negative aspect of Khrushchev's years was probably his antireligious campaign, aimed at the wholesale destruction of religious life in the country. In the process, half of all Orthodox churches, 80 percent of all synagogues, and two-thirds of all mosques were either destroyed or locked up. Catholics in Lithuania, Latvia, and western Ukraine were hit especially hard.

Khrushchev's record in the area of nationality policy was mixed: progressive when it came to human rights, his policies were regressive on matters of language and religious rights. Khrushchev never took the issue of national autonomy very seriously. He saw the Soviet federal system as being on its way to oblivion, having served its purpose, rather than as a genuine partnership, or at least a serviceable one that ought not to be tampered with, if only out of Kremlin self-interest.

7

Brezhnev's Peace and Prosperity

If Stalin's era laid the foundation of Soviet nationality policy, Brezhnev's era of "developed socialism," later so derided, brought it to its fruition. Brezhnev's era was the culmination of what Soviet nationality policy and the socialist economy were capable of delivering.

The organized displacement of human masses (the last being Khrushchev's dispatch of hundreds of thousands of settlers to the Virgin Lands of northern Kazakhstan) had ended. The party apparatus in the national republics no longer lived in fear of purges or reformist campaigns. Even better, local party bosses were allowed free rein on their own turf. Russian "colonial" apparatchiks were less watchdogs than cooperative partners. Brezhnev was obviously a partisan of "live and let live": as long as the Kremlin's rule went unchallenged and proper tribute was forwarded, local elites were allowed to pocket all the benefits they could extract under this "laissez faire" version of "developed socialism."

Prosperous party cliques developed in practically all the republics, operating under the wings of powerful party secretaries: Dinmukhamed Kunaev in Kazakhstan, Sharaf Rashidov in Uzbekistan, Heydar Aliev in Azerbaijan, Vladimir Shcherbitsky in the Ukraine, and others. The new prosperity benefited the lower social echelons as well: they were allowed to sell influence, protection, and contacts; to enjoy the comforts of conformity; and to approximate "bourgeois" standards of living. These benefits accelerated the formation of a Soviet middle class, probably the key achievement of the period. Managers of industry, commerce, and agriculture shared in this new prosperity. In turn, money was flowing from the republics to Moscow in the form of kickbacks to central officials either for favors or simply for noninterference.

The slogan "Friendship among peoples" appeared to be the rule, but it was grounded in pragmatism rather than ideology. Occasional instances of ethnic violence (for example, the Tashkent stadium riot of 1969) were dismissed as hooliganism. Some past injustices (e.g., the exile of the Meskhetians, the Volga Germans, and the Crimean Tatars) were left unremedied. Anti-Semitism became fashionable and provided a convenient outlet for every sort of local discontent, and Jewish quotas were established in education and employment.

Leonid Brezhnev clearly saw Russia as the imperial nation, entitled to a leading role in the Union; but because he was a compromiser by temperament and necessity, he was willing and ready to share the benefits of "developed socialism" with local Party elites on "their own" territories as long as the Kremlin's ultimate control went unchallenged.

This ethnic peace, despite its obvious shortcomings, fostered the development of a new generation of native managers and intellectuals. A genuine middle class appeared, undisturbed by Lenin's revolutionary visions, Stalin's social engineering, or Khrushchev's reformist zeal. The new elites, while conformist and politically docile, were confident of their rights and privileges. When Gorbachev arrived on the scene with his ambitious ideas of modernization and reforms, the elites of Brezhnev's era provided cadres for the competing sides. Some clung to the old, others endorsed change. Still others, seeing the power of the center diminish, sought to reinforce their local influence through nationalist appeals, sometimes even leading their nations toward independence.

Lenin demolished the old imperial order and Stalin established a new one, but Brezhnev offered the fruits of empire to be enjoyed for the first time, in peace. This was the very best the regime could offer. Its achievements impressed enough Western scholars that they argued about the need to study "the success of Soviet nationality policies." But the nationality policy of the USSR had run its course, as events would soon show.

8

The Rupture of the
Modus Vivendi

The first rupture of Brezhnev's "live and let live" approach took place during the short tenure of Yuri Andropov. The former KGB chief had a thorough knowledge of the corruption and malfunctioning of the Brezhnev system, especially in the southern republics, and he set out to clean things up. Thus began a four-year purge which shook the Party nomenklatura in several republics, dislodging numerous Party leaders and their cliques, and "parachuting" Russian outsiders in to take command. The newcomers were selected the way kolkhoz chairmen had been chosen during collectivization, the main qualification being a reasonable degree of reliability and no ties to the local population, thus diminishing the opportunity for nepotism. At the same time, younger and as yet uncompromised native cadres were promoted to replace the coteries of purged leaders.

Initially, these measures seemed to be relatively effective, especially in the eyes of outside observers, who based their judgment on the ranks and numbers of purged officials. The brief tenure of the colorless Konstantin Chernenko after Andropov's death did not stop the process, which had acquired its own momentum. With Chernenko's own speedy death and the arrival of Gorbachev, another shuffling of cadres took place, with a wholesale replacement of incumbents by Gorbachev's own nominees.

Among Gorbachev's first attempts to change Soviet life was an anti-alcohol campaign. This had been begun by Andropov but was carried on with renewed fervor by Gorbachev as a means to promote sobriety, discipline, and productivity. As a result, Slavic vodka drinkers, suffering from the reduced supply and higher prices, turned to home distilling and to drinking anything alcoholic. The wine lovers of the southern belt were forced to uproot thousands of acres of vineyards, a destruction that will require years to undo. The southerners considered the measure unjust, as it made them pay for the northern proclivity for strong drink. The campaign failed to reduce drunkenness, interfered with other reform measures, and brought economic hardship. It withered away amidst public discontent, as would be the fate of most of Gorbachev's reforms to come.

Thus, obstacles to Gorbachev's plans for improvement began to appear at the very outset and increased at each attempt to implement change. In Central Asia and the Transcaucasus the inefficiency and corruption that Andropov and Gorbachev so deplored were not simply features of oriental tradition, they were a way of making the system function. Anticorruption measures brought havoc to an economy in which corruption had been a prime motivator and shady deals had been the way to circumvent bureaucratic red tape. Personal initiative, so essential for keeping the economy moving, could only function through illegal or semilegal channels. Moreover, local party bosses, old and new alike, saw the freedom to milk their "fiefdoms" as part and parcel of the "gentlemen's agreement" with Moscow, a price paid by the latter for their collaboration.

The policy of "parachuting" in Russian apparatchiks to break up local fiefdoms lost legitimacy in the context of Gorbachev's liberalization drive with its slogans of *glasnost* and *demokratizatsiia*. Many formerly purged native officials resurfaced and alleged that they had suffered from national discrimination. Corruption, they said, had been forced on them by Moscow bosses who demanded payoffs and kickbacks.

These old apparatchiks found a sympathetic ear among those

conservative elements in the Kremlin who were eager to restore the old *modus vivendi:* the old-timers were used to political obedience (at a price), and provided electoral and parliamentary support to conservatives willing to pay that price. In the March 1989 elections to the USSR Supreme Soviet, Communists won 87 percent of the seats, despite impressive losses in Moscow, Leningrad, Sverdlovsk, and the Baltic republics. The bulk of the country, and especially the Muslim republics, followed the lead of Party bosses and voted in the official candidates.

Considering himself a relatively tolerant, sophisticated, modern thinker, a rational man open to compromise, Gorbachev had little inkling of the tensions simmering below the surface of the "friendship of peoples." The allegiance of local elites to the Kremlin and the dependence of the national republics on Moscow were presumed to be permanent. Thus when Gorbachev turned his full attention to reconstruction of the national economy and the battle against bureaucratic resistance to reform, he gave little thought to possible negative repercussions in the relations between the republics and the center. But as fear of the Kremlin declined and glasnost untied people's tongues, Party leaders in the republics were forced to seek grass-roots support. In the Baltic republics the need to respond to resurgent national feelings became so great that it undermined relations with Moscow. In the other republics, especially in the Muslim areas, the local Party apparatus sought to enhance its legitimacy by extracting more freedom for Islam, without pressing for wider political autonomy. In the Caucasus, nationalist sentiments surfaced at the first opportunity, fueling interethnic conflicts and creating centrifugal drives.

Gorbachev, unable to keep nationality issues out of the way, was faced with conflicting needs to advance his liberalizing reforms without relinquishing central control. He saw limited national revival in the republics as a potential asset in combating conservative resistance to change, but failed to realize that, once in motion, such forces could not be prevented from taking the road toward national self-determination.

Wishing to heal, not replace, the system, Gorbachev opted for gradual liberalization. The national republics were allowed increased say in their own affairs, but without a diminution of central prerogative. The motto was to "strengthen both the republics and the center"—another exercise in dialectical wishful thinking.

Among possible areas where local control could be extended, the cultural field appeared least dangerous to the center, and concessions were made in the areas of education, use of local languages, publication of previously prohibited works, and freedom of the press in general. In the political sphere, Gorbachev gradually accepted the return to traditional national symbols (flags, anthems, shields, city and street names), but tried to slow down the transition to effective self-government. He was, however, willing to unload on the republics a whole array of costly social programs that mostly benefited the southern republics with their high birthrates. Nevertheless, he remained reluctant to loosen Moscow's grip on all-Union enterprises, budget allocations, and taxation.

The incompleteness of the reform agenda, with its half-steps aimed at revitalizing a moribund system and its tantalizing concessions to nationalities coupled with a determination to keep intact the territorial legacy of the Romanov empire, led to bloody ethnic confrontations in the republics. Alma-Ata, Tbilisi, Baku, Dushanbe, Vilnius—each episode of violence eroded the Union. The inexorable evolution of the Baltic republics toward independence presented Gorbachev with a most difficult dilemma: either to separate their case from the others by using the repudiation of the Molotov-Ribbentrop agreement as a loophole, or to hold on to the three republics and so dissuade others from trying to follow suit. Gorbachev chose a middle road: he allowed the Baltic republics to gain almost complete *de facto* sovereignty but maintained the Soviet military occupation in order to prevent their exit from the Union. The result was that both the Baltic nationalists and the Soviet conservatives perceived Gorbachev as their enemy for exactly opposite reasons.

Gorbachev was caught in the fundamental dilemma that faces every reformer: the choice between self-preservation and promoting genuine change, which inevitably brings with it unintended, and usually uncontrollable, consequences. He aimed for a middle course, trying to manage all the opposing interests. The military-industrial complex, the heaviest burden on the national economy and a primary foe of the sovereignty of national republics, could not easily be controlled. It favored strong central authority and supported the conservative forces opposed to reforms. The liberal forces, indispensable to the success of reform, were inevitably prone to undermine the authority of the center. Gorbachev constantly maneuvered between the two competing camps, alternately favoring one side over the other and presenting himself as a lesser evil for each side.

Toward the end of 1990 and into the spring of 1991, as nationalist forces gained strength in the republics and some of Gorbachev's liberal allies grew impatient with his temporizing, he made a desperate attempt to court the conservatives. Abandoning his reformist supporters, he brought into his team a number of old Party bureaucrats, among them Gennadii Yanaev, who was elected at Gorbachev's request to the specially created position of vice-president. But Gorbachev's hope of coopting the conservatives without abandoning his reforms failed: not only did the reform process come to a halt, but the conservative forces aimed directly at erasing all his achievements.

By the summer of 1991 it appeared that Gorbachev was once again ready to change course, this time in the direction of liberalization. His March 1991 referendum on a new Union Treaty that would give substantial rights to the republics won the approval of 76 percent of the Soviet population. The treaty lost only in the small independence-minded republics that wanted nothing short of secession. But the Kremlin conservatives were opposed to all concessions. One day prior to the scheduled signing of the treaty, on August 19, 1991, leaders of the party, the security forces, and the military-industrial complex, backed by a few generals, organized a putsch. The country was to be reset on a conservative course, with law and order restored, renegade republics brought to heel, and communist ideology resanctified. Gorbachev was to be coopted or eliminated. Through a combination of chance, miscalculation, and unexpected resistance on the part of democratic forces led by the president of the Russian Republic, Boris Yeltsin, the putsch ran out of steam. The reluctance of assault units to storm the "White House," headquarters of the government of Russia and the command center of the resistance, led to the collapse of the junta within 72 hours.

Gorbachev, freed from house arrest but chastened by his experience, had no choice but to share power with his rescuer, Russia's elected president. Soon it became clear that he had no power to share, as one by one the republics asserted their independence. His proposed Union Treaty fell into oblivion, and was replaced in December 1991 by a loose "Commonwealth of Independent States." On January 1, 1992, the red flag was hauled down from Kremlin's towers and the Russian tricolor raised in its place. The Soviet Union was no longer, and Gorbachev had nothing over which to preside.

9

Yeltsin and the Nationalities

During his struggle against the nomenklatura-led central government in the last years of the USSR, Boris Yeltsin, Russia's first elected president, championed the sovereignty of the republics against the authority of the center. He supported the right of every union republic to secede at will, and condemned all central attempts to hold the Union together by military force. In taking such a stand, Yeltsin earned the gratitude of many non-Russian leaders.

Now that the union republics have become independent states, with membership in the United Nations and in other international organizations, they confront Russia with a new kind of foreign-policy challenge: relations with what Russians now call the "near abroad." A complicating factor is the fate of the substantial Russian populations residing the former Soviet republics. The Russian settlers, suddenly deprived of their "leading nation" status, are now themselves in the position of national minorities and look to Russia for support in their dealings with local authorities. This presents Yeltsin with a difficult dilemma: to defer to the sovereignty of the new states, even if Russian minorities there are aggrieved, or to "defend" the Russians, endangering those relations. (There is some irony in the fact that during the August 1991 events, Baltic nationalists backed Yeltsin while the Russian interfronts and unions of labor collectives backed the junta.)

190

Table 23

Russians in the Former Soviet Union (1989 census)

Republic(s)	Russian population (millions)	% Russian
Russian Federation	119.9	81.5
Ukraine	11.4	22.1
Belarus	1.3	13.2
Kazakhstan	6.2	37.8
Central Asia (4 republics)	3.3	10.1
Baltic (3 republics)	1.7	19.0
Transcaucasia (3 republics)	0.8	5.1
Moldova	0.6	13.0

Source: Institute of Ethnology and Anthropology, Russian Academy of Sciences, *Russkie: Sotsiologicheskie ocherki* (Moscow: Nauka, 1992), pp. 93, 96–97.

Note: The Central Asian republics are Kyrgyzstan, Tajikistan, Turkmenistan, and Uzbekistan; the Baltic: Estonia, Latvia, and Lithuania; and the Transcaucasian: Armenia, Azerbaijan, and Georgia.

In their turn, the autonomous republics *within* the Russian Federation are also demanding various degrees of sovereignty. But for Russia to accept the right of the autonomous republics to secede would not be a simple matter. Many are islands within Russian territory (for example, the Tatar and Bashkir republics). Other nations are not very numerous and even constitute a minority within their own territories, with Russians being in the overwhelming majority. Under such circumstances, Yeltsin has little choice but to deny the republics of the Russian Federation the rights he himself supported for the union republics. This, in turn, prompts the leaders of the "autonomous" national units to speak of continued Russian colonialism and to ignore Moscow directives, while Russian nationalists pressure Yeltsin to apply a firm hand in dealing with secessionist demands. The strong showing of Vladimir Zhirinovsky and his party in the December 1993 parliamentary elections must command the attention of the Russian government—and of Russia's neighbors.

Still, Yeltsin has been reluctant to use force in disputes with

Table 24

Russian Population in Component Republics of the Russian Federation (1989)

Republic	Russian population (%)
Adyge[a]	68
Bashkortostan (Bashkiria)	39
Buryatia	70
Chechnia (incl. Ingushetia)[b]	22
Chuvashia	27
Dagestan	9
Ingushetia[b]	(see Chechnia)
Kabardino-Balkaria	32
Khalmg Tanch (Kalmykia)	38
Karachai-Cherkess[a]	42
Karelia	74
Khakassia[a]	80[c]
Komi	58
Mari	48
Mordovian	61
Mountain Altai[a]	65
North Ossetia	30
Sakha (Yakutia)	50
Tatarstan	43
Tuva	32
Udmurtia	59

Source: 1989 census.
[a]Upgraded from the status of autonomous region after the demise of the USSR.
[b]Split in 1992.
[c]1979 census.

either the newly independent republics or those located within the borders of the Russian Federation, such as the Chechen Republic, which declared its independence after the failure of the Moscow putsch in 1991. He has appeared willing, for example, to negotiate a treaty with the Volga Tatars that would grant Tatarstan semi-independent status within the Russian Federation. When pressure needs to be applied, Yeltsin prefers to work through pro-Moscow factions in the republics or to use economic sanctions.

The new Russian constitution drafted by the Yeltsin government and approved in the December 1993 referendum (which some of the republics boycotted) provides for a strong presidency and a weak legislature elected according to a new system. The new parliament, called a Federal Assembly, is made up of two chambers. The upper house is a Federation Council made up of two representatives from each of the 89 units making up the Russian Federation, including republics as well as regions and territories. One of the powers reserved to the upper house is the power to confirm internal boundary changes. The 450 members of the lower house, the State Duma, are chosen under a complicated system in which half the seats are apportioned to parties based on their nationwide share of the vote while the other half are directly elected from individual districts.

One striking innovation of the new constitution is that it grants as much autonomy to Russia's regions as to its republics. Also notable is the fact that no provision is made for the withdrawal of component units from the federation. The key tenet of Yeltsin's strategy on the nationality issue has been that of economic self-interest. Russia will no longer subsidize either foreign clients or former Soviet republics. Thus no money for Cuba or Angola, but by the same token no cheap energy for Lithuania or cheap lumber for Ukraine. Russia prefers to trade on an equal basis, either through barter or for hard currency. Retrenchment within Russian borders combined with priority for Russian interests has been the basis of Yeltsin's approach. The assumption is that once Russia recovers from her present economic difficulties, the very weight of Russia's natural wealth and the size of the Russian market will compel her neighbors to recognize Russia's preeminence and adjust their policies to Moscow's liking without any military pressure.

In this sense, Yeltsin is in a race against time: the longer it takes for the Russian economy to show signs of health and the population to regain some sense of material well-being, the greater will be the potential for the forces of reaction to succeed in their quest for power.

Conclusion

All the former union republics of the Soviet Union are now independent, with their own governments, leaders, flags, anthems, currencies, customs, and most of all, problems. The transition to independence has been rough: reborn national aspirations have clashed with economic and demographic realities; the road away from Soviet-style socialism has been uphill; and early hopes for immediate change have been thwarted by the realization that things will undoubtedly get much worse before even starting on the road to improvement. Western aid, an eagerly awaited compensation for abandoning the communist path, has fallen short of expectations. Existing socioeconomic conditions and entrenched attitudes and habits carried over from decades of communist rule have proved to be serious obstacles to market reforms.

The changes that have taken place, while generally supported by the intelligentsia, have left whole layers of the communist apparatus in place for the simple reason that there appeared to be no alternative to transitional bureaucratic management and no one else to run the bureaucratic machinery. And indeed, many apparatchiks quite readily embraced both nationalist credos and the rhetoric of market reform; after all, it was no secret that communist ideology had been dead for decades. Yet the new ideological commitments seemed to go no deeper than the old.

The real preoccupation of the run of officials, bureaucrats, and managers has ever been to maintain, and preferably to enhance, their own power and privileges. Thus, the "market" was perceived as freedom to implement price hikes, not as an opening to competition, while "privatization" seemed to promise legitimation for the acquisition of wealth by entrenched insiders.

Throughout the former Soviet Union, the communist bureaucrats, the new democratically elected officeholders, and the burgeoning mafia structures all in one way or another profit from the economic crisis and have a certain interest in prolonging it. To that end, they want to ensure that any movement away from the command-and-control system and toward a competitive market economy is slow and cautious and does not endanger their positions (and earning ability).

Since the euphoria of the early days of newly acquired independence and the downfall of communism, the post-Soviet republics have had to face reality: economic deterioration, social chaos, continued dependence on Russian energy and raw materials, insufficient Western aid, a scarcity of qualified elites other than those who came up through the communist ranks, and the challenge of preserving an orderly way of life under democratic conditions. Russia, despite its weakening state, is still capable of holding its former possessions within its sphere of interest. Russia's substantial military might and natural wealth, its position as potential arbiter in interethnic conflicts, as well as the durability of old economic ties, weigh in Moscow's favor.

What is the future of the fifteen states that have succeeded the Soviet Union? Can they survive as independent states? Will Russia try to recover any of them? Will some drift into the orbit of neighboring powers, attracted by common culture, religion, and history? No one can predict for sure, but some trends have already emerged.

1. After achieving their independence, the new post-Soviet states have encountered more difficulties than they ever an-

ticipated. In some cases widespread disillusionment has led to electoral defeats of nationalist parties. On the positive side, to the extent that these difficulties favor the emergence of a Russia-led common market, the result might be a lessening of national tensions.

2. The widely expected growth of Turkish influence on the Turkic-speaking former Soviet republics seems to be limited to the cultural sphere. Turkey has been cautious in its eastern policy. It abstained from interfering in the Azeri-Armenian conflict and has exercised little political influence on developments in Central Asia. Iranian inroads in Azerbaijan (common religion) and Tajikistan (common language) have been more daring; but Iran, like Turkey, is constrained by the need to respect Russia's interests.

3. The attraction of East–Central Europe, especially of Poland, has been mitigated in Ukraine and Belarus by the reality of continuous economic dependence on Russia. Poland, for its part, has shown itself to be as careful as Turkey: notwithstanding its active *Ostpolitik*, Warsaw is keenly aware of its own economic and military limitations and is not interested in challenging Moscow.

4. Moscow's post-Soviet policy toward the former union republics has already emerged: it bears a remarkable similarity to America's Monroe Doctrine, admitting no foreign interference within its sphere of influence. Thus, along the Tajik-Afghan border, Russian border guards "defend Russia's security." In the Caucasus, Russia has reverted to a divide-and-rule policy, using Armenia as the linchpin of its influence (as in the nineteenth century). Russia lurks behind some of the ethnic turmoil in Georgia and Azerbaijan, even as it positions itself in the arbiter role. Moscow uses Ukraine's dependence on Russian energy and mineral resources to forestall her westward political slide. In the Baltic republics, the predicament of Russian minorities is being skillfully exploited by Moscow, which would prefer to have that region strategically "finlandized."

Moscow has lost its empire but not its imperial consciousness. While resigned to total independence for its former East European satellites, Moscow has shown a clear intention to maintain a commanding position among the former component republics of the USSR. This includes pulling the weak economies of the post-Soviet states into the ruble zone, being sole heir to the Soviet nuclear arsenal, serving as the arbiter of regional and interethnic conflicts, and, most important of all, keeping outside powers from encroaching on Russia's sphere of influence.

Selected Bibliography

Agursky, M. *Ideologiia natsional-bolshevizma*. Paris: YMCA Press, 1980.

Akademiia nauk SSSR. Institut Etnografii. *Sovremennye etnicheskie protsessy v SSSR*. Moscow: Nauka, 1975.

Allworth, Edward. *The Modern Uzbeks*. Stanford: Hoover Press, 1990.

———. *Nationality Group Survival in Multi-Ethnic States*. New York: Praeger, 1977.

——— (ed.). *Ethnic Russia in the USSR. The Dilemma of Dominance*. Elmsford, NY: Pergamon, 1980.

——— (ed.). *The Nationality Question in Soviet Central Asia*. New York–London: Praeger, 1973.

Alstadt, Audrey L. *The Azerbaijani Turks: Power and Identity Under the Russian Rule*. Stanford: Hoover Press, 1992.

Amalrik, Andrei. *Will the Soviet Union Survive Until 1984?* New York: Praeger, 1978

Armstrong, John A. *Ukrainian Nationalism*. 2nd ed. Englewood, CO: Libraries Unlimited, 1980.

Azrael, Jeremy (ed.). *Soviet Nationality Policy and Practice*. New York–London: Praeger, 1978.

Bahry, Donna. *Outside Moscow: Power, Politics, and Budgetary Policy in the Soviet Union*. New York: Columbia University Press, 1987.

Bennigsen, Alexandre, and Lemercier-Quelquejay, Chantal. *Islam in the Soviet Union*. New York–London: Praeger, 1967.

Bennigsen, Alexandre, and Wimbush, Enders S. *Muslims of the Soviet Empire: A Guide*. Bloomington: Indiana University Press, 1986.

———. *Muslim Communism in the Soviet Union*. Chicago: University of Chicago Press, 1979.

Bennigsen-Broxup, Marie (ed.). *The North Caucasus Barrier: The Russian Advances Towards the Muslim World*. New York: St. Martin's Press, 1992.

Besançon, Alain. *Present soviétique et passé russe*. Paris: Le livre de poche, 1980.

Besemeres, John F. *Socialist Population Politics: The Political Implications of Demographic Trends in the USSR and Eastern Europe.* Armonk, NY: M.E. Sharpe, 1980.

Bremmer, Ian, and Taras, Ray (eds.). *Nations and Politics in the Soviet Successor States.* New York and Cambridge: Cambridge University Press, 1993.

Bromlei, Iu.V. *Ocherki teorii etnosa.* Moscow: Nauka, 1983.

Bruk, S.I. *Naselenie mira. Etnodemograficheskii spravochnik.* Moscow: Nauka, 1986.

Butino, Marco (ed.). *Underdevelopment, Ethnic Conflicts, and Nationalisms in the Soviet Union.* Proceedings of the Seventh International Colloqium, Cortona, Italy, May 1991. Milano: Fondazione Giangiacomo Feltrinelli, 1993.

Carrère d'Encausse, Hélène. *L'Empire éclaté.* Paris: Flammarion, 1978.

―――. *La Gloire de nations ou la fin de l'empire soviétique.* Paris: Fayard, 1980.

―――. *Ni paix ni guerre. Le Nouvel Empire soviétique ou le bon usage de la détente.* Paris: Flammarion, 1987.

―――. *Le Pouvoir confisqué. Gouvernants et gouvernés en URSS.* Paris: Flammarion, 1980.

Conquest, Robert (ed.). *The Last Empire: Nationality and the Soviet Future.* Stanford: Hoover Press, 1986.

Critchlow, James. *Nationalism in Uzbekistan: A Soviet Republic's Road to Sovereignty.* Boulder, CO: Westview Press, 1992.

Dmytryshin, Basil. *Moscow and the Ukraine, 1918–1953.* New York: Brookman, 1956.

Dziuba, Ivan. *Internationalism and Russification: A Study in the Soviet Nationality Problems.* 2nd ed. London: Weidenfield and Nicholson, 1968.

Gleason, Gregory. *Federalism and Nationalism: The Struggle for Republican Rights in the USSR.* Boulder, CO: Westview Press, 1990.

Fierman, William (ed.). *Soviet Central Asia: The Failed Transformation.* Boulder, CO: Westview Press, 1991.

Friedberg, Maurice, and Isham, Heyward (eds.). *Soviet Society Under Gorbachev.* Armonk, NY: M.E. Sharpe, 1987.

Frumkina, Ia.G. et al. (eds.). *Kniga o russkom evreistve.* New York: Soiuz russkikh evreev, 1968.

Guboglo, Mikhail. "Demography and Language in the Capitals of the Union Republics." *Journal of Soviet Nationalities,* vol. 1, no. 4 (Winter 1990–91).

―――. *Sovremennye etnoiazykovye protsessy v SSSR. Osnovnye faktory i tendentsii razvitiia natsional'no-russkogo dvuiazychiia.* Moscow: Nauka, 1984.

Hajda, Lubomir, and Bessinger, Mark (eds.). *The Nationalities Factor in Soviet Politics and Society.* Boulder, CO: Westview Press, 1990.

Hayit, Baymirza. *Islam and Turkestan Under Russian Rule.* Istanbul, 1987.

Huttenbach, Henry R. (ed). *Soviet Nationality Policies: Ruling Ethnic Groups in the USSR.* London: Mansell, 1990.

Huttenbach, Henry, and Motyl, Alexander (eds.). Proceedings of conferences sponsored by the Program on Nationalities and Siberian Studies. The Harriman Institute for Advanced Study of the Soviet Union, Columbia University. Special issues of *Nationalities Papers*, 1989–92: "The Soviet Nationalities and Gorbachev" (Spring 1989); "The Soviet Nationalities Against Gorbachev" (Spring 1990); "The Soviet Nationalities Despite Gorbachev" (Spring 1991); "The Soviet Nationalities Without Gorbachev" (Spring 1992).

Karklins, Rasma. *Ethnic Relations in the USSR*. Boston: Allen & Unwin, 1986.

Kohn, Hans (ed.). *The Mind of Modern Russia: Historical and Political Thoughts of Russia's Great Age*. New York: Harper Brothers, 1955.

Koyre, Alexandre. *La Philosophie et le problème national en Russie au debut du XIX siecle*. Paris: Gallimard, 1976.

Kozlov, Viktor. "Natsional'nyi separatizm ili kazhdomu svoe," *Moskva*, 1991, no. 11.

———. *The Peoples of the Soviet Union*. Bloomington: Indiana University Press, 1988.

Kublak, Heronim et al. (eds.). *Mniejszosci polskie i Polonia w ZSSR*. Wroclaw: Uniwersytet Jagiellonski. Instytut badan polonistycznych, 1992.

Lemercier-Quelquejay, Chantal et al. (eds.). *Etudes offertes à Alexandre Bennigsen. Passé Turco-Tatar. Présent soviétique*. Louvain-Paris: Editions Peters, 1986.

Lewickyi, Boris. *Polityka narodowosciowa ZSSR w dobie Chruszczowa*. Paris: Instytut Literacki, 1966.

Lubin, Nancy. *Labor and Nationality in Soviet Central Asia*. Princeton: Princeton University Press, 1985.

Mandelbaum, Michael (ed.). *The Rise of Nations in the Soviet Union*. New York: Council on Foreign Relations, 1991.

Misiunas, Romuald J., and Taagepera, Rein. *The Baltic States: Years of Dependence, 1940–1980*. Berkeley: University of California Press, 1983.

Motyl, Alexander I. *Will the Non-Russians Rebel? State, Ethnicity, and Stability in the USSR*. New York: Cornell University Press, 1987.

——— (ed.). *The Post Soviet Nations: Perspectives on the Demise of the USSR*. New York: Columbia University Press, 1922.

——— (ed.). *Thinking Theoretically About Soviet Nationalities*. New York: Columbia University Press, 1992.

Nahaylo, Bohdan, and Swoboda, Victor. *Soviet Disunion: A History of the Nationalities Problem in the USSR*. London: Hamish Hamilton, 1990.

Nationalism in the USSR: Problems of Nationalism. Amsterdam: Second World Center, 1989.

Nolde, Boris. *La Formation de l'Empire Russe. Etudes, notes, et documents*. 2 vols. Paris: Institut d'Etudes Slaves, 1952–53.

Olcott, Martha B. *The Kazakhs*. Stanford: The Hoover Press, 1987.

——— (ed.). *The Soviet Multinational State: Readings and Documents*. Armonk, NY: M.E. Sharpe, 1987.

Pap, Michael S. (ed.). *Russian Empire. Some Aspects of Tsarist and Soviet Colonial Practices*. Cleveland: Institute for Soviet and East European Studies, John Carroll University, Ukrainian Historical Society, 1985.

Perevedentsev, Viktor. *Molodezh' i sotsial'no-demograficheskie problemy.* Moscow: Nauka, 1990 [and other brochures by the same author].

Pinkus, Benjamin. *The Jews of the Soviet Union. A History of a National Minority.* New York: Cambridge University Press, 1988.

Ra'anan, Uri, and Perry, Charles M. (eds.). *The USSR Today and Tomorrow. Problems and Challenges.* Lexington–Toronto: Lexington Books, 1987.

Ramet, Pedro (ed.). *Religion and Nationalism in Soviet and East European Politics.* Durham, NC: Duke University Press, 1984.

Rorlich, Azade-Ayse. *The Volga Tatars.* Stanford: The Hoover Press, 1986.

Rossiiskaia Akademiia Nauk. Institut etnologii i antropologii. *Russkie. Etno-sotsiologicheskie ocherki.* Moscow: Nauka, 1992.

Rumer, Boris Z. *Soviet Central Asia: "A Tragic Experiment."* Boston: Unwin Hyman, 1989.

Rywkin, Michael. *Moscow's Muslim Challenge: Soviet Central Asia.* 2nd ed. Armonk, NY: M.E. Sharpe, 1990.

———. *Soviet Society Today.* Armonk, NY: M.E. Sharpe, 1989.

——— (ed.). *Russian Colonial Expansion to 1917.* London: Mansell, 1988.

Saidbaev, T.S. *Islam i obshchestvo.* Moscow: Nauka, 1978.

"Samaia politicheskaia karta SSSR." *Moskovskie novosti,* 1991, no. 11 (March 17).

Schwartz, Lee. "USSR: Nationality Redistribution by Republic, 1979–1989." *Soviet Geography,* vol. 32, no. 4 (April 1991).

Shkaratan, Ovsei. "Ethnic and Nationality Problems and Conflicts in Etacratic Society." Colloquium on "Capitalism and Democracy," University of California in Los Angeles, March 1991 [unpublished].

——— (ed.). *NTR i natsional'nye protsessy.* Moscow: Nauka, 1987.

Shlapentokh, Vladimir et al. (eds.). *The New Russian Diaspora.* Armonk, NY: M.E. Sharpe, 1994.

Silnitskii, Frantishek. "Natsional'naia politika SSSR v period s 1917 po 1922 god." Munich: Suchastnist', 1978.

Simon, Gerhard. *Nationalism and Policy Towards the Nationalities in the Soviet Union.* Boulder, CO: Westview Press, 1991.

Solzhenitsyn, A.I. "Kak nam obustroit Rossiiu. Posil'nye sobrazheniia." *Literaturnaia gazeta,* September 18, 1990.

Subtelny, Orest. *Ukraine: A History.* Toronto: University of Toronto Press, 1988.

Suny, Ronald G. *The Making of the Georgian Nation.* Bloomington: Indiana University Press, 1988.

——— (ed.). *Transcaucasia: Nationalism and Social Change. Essays in the History of Armenia, Azerbaijan, and Georgia.* Ann Arbor: Michigan Slavic Publications, 1983.

Szporluk, Roman. *Communism and Nationalism: Karl Marx versus Friedrich List.* New York: Oxford University Press, 1991.

Tokarev, S.A. *Etnografiia narodov SSSR.* Moscow: Izdatel'stvo Moskovskogo universiteta, 1958.

Topilin, A.V. "The Territorial Redistribution of Labor Resources in the USSR." *Problems of Economics,* May 1980.

Trembicki, W. "Flags of Non-Russian Peoples Under Soviet Rule," *The Flag Bulletin,* vol. 8, no. 3 (1969).
Voslensky, Michael. *Nomenklatura: The Soviet Ruling Class.* New York: Doubleday, 1984.
Wheeler, Geoffrey. *The Modern History of Central Asia.* New York: Praeger, 1964.
Wimbush, Enders S. *Soviet Nationalities in Strategic Perspective.* New York: St. Martin's Press, 1985.
Wixman, Ronald. *The Peoples of the USSR: An Ethnographic Handbook.* Armonk, NY: M.E. Sharpe, 1984.
Yanov, Alexander. *The Russian New Right.* Berkeley: University of California, 1978.
Zaslavsky, Victor. *The Neo-Stalinist State: Class, Ethnicity, and Consensus in Soviet Society.* Armonk, NY: M.E. Sharpe, 1994 (rev. ed.).

Journals

Argumenty i fakty
Canadian Slavonic Papers
Central Asian Survey
Etnopolis
Istoriia SSSR (now: *Otechestvennaia istoriia*)
Journal of Soviet Nationalities
Nationalities Papers
Raduga
Revue du monde russe et soviétique
Report on the USSR (now: *Report on Eurasia*)
RFE/RL Research Reports
Russian Review
Sovetskaia etnografiia (now: *Etnograficheskoe obozrenie*)
Soviet Studies (now: *Europe-Asia Studies*)
Vestnik statistiki
Voprosy istorii

Index

About the Author

Michael Rywkin, born in eastern Poland, spent several years in Central Asia as a World War II refugee and attended the Uzbek State University in Samarkand for one year. Subsequently educated in France and the United States, he completed a doctorate in political science at Columbia University.

Currently Professor Emeritus of Russian Area Studies at the City College of New York, Rywkin is also president of the Association for the Study of Nationalities (ex-USSR and Eastern Europe). During frequent trips to the former Soviet Union over the past decade, he has visited the cities of Baku, Bukhara, Erevan, Khiva, Kiev, Leningrad (now St. Petersburg), Moscow, Samarkand, Tallinn, Tartu, Tashkent, Tbilisi, and Vilnius.

Rywkin is the author of *Soviet Society Today* (M.E. Sharpe, 1989), *Moscow's Muslim Challenge* (M.E. Sharpe, 1990, rev. ed.), and editor of the volume *Russian Colonial Expansion to 1917*.